Kich

CATS

CATS

COLLINS · Glasgow and London

ANIMAL
WORLD
SERIES
General Editor
David Stephen

G. P. PUTNAM'S SONS · New York

Acknowledgements

Page 10: J. Burton-Photo Researchers; 11(above): J. Markham; 11(below): J. Simon-Photo Researchers; 12: Okapia; 13: W. Lummer; 14(above): Bavaria-A. Thau; 14(below): Aarons; 15(above): E. Muench-Ostman; 15(below): Fievet-Jacana; 16(above): S. Trevor-Photo Researchers; 16(below): N. Cirani; 17: Visage-Jacana; 18–19: N. Cirani; 20: N. Myers-Photo Researchers; 21: Richter; 22: Des Bartlett-Photo Researchers; 23: B. Barbey-Magnum; 24: Fievet-Jacana; 25: D. Patterson-Photo Researchers; 26(above): Fievet-Jacana; 26(below): N. Cirani; 27: Fievet-Jacana; 28: Fievet-Jacana; 29: F. Petter-Afrique Photo; 30-1: Visage-Jacana; 31: L. Pellegrini; 32-3: Okapia; 34: Ylla-Rapho; 35: Brake-Rapho; 36: Okapia; 38-9: Prenzel-Press; 40: W. Suschitzky; 41: D. Robinson; 42: F. Peter-Jacana; 43(above): Time Life; 43(below, both): Quilici; 44(above): Aarons; 44(below): Margiocco; 45: Russ Kine-Photo Researchers; 46: Klages-Atlas Photo; 47: Comet; 48: Aarons; 49: Aarons; 50: Time Life; 51(above): Visage-Jacana; 51(below): Okapia; 52: Milan Zoo; 53(left): I. Berry-Magnum; 53(right): Time Life; 54: Time Life; 55: Time Life; 56(above): Dragesco-Atlas Photo; 56(below): Fievet-Jacana; 57: Klages-Atlas Photo; 58-9: Blomstrand-Jacana; 60: Visage-Jacana; 61: Okapia; 62(left): Aarons; 62(right): Dragesco-Atlas Photo; 63: Atlantic Press; 64-5: Atlantic Press; 66: Klages-Atlas Photo; 67(both): Parbst-Rapho and Atlantic Press; 68: Klages-Atlas Photo; 69: R. Allin; 70: F. Lane; 71(above): E. A. Heiniger; 71(below): A. Visage-Jacana; 72: A. Visage-Jacana; 73: Lee Rue; 74(above): Prenzel Press; 74(below): W. Lummer; 75(above): Prenzel Press; 75(below): Zuber Rapho; 76: A. Fatras; 77: E. A. Heiniger; 78-9: D. Robinson-Photo Researchers; 80: Des Bartlett-Denis Productions; 81(above): A. Visage-Jacana; 81(below): A. Fatras; 82: Okapia; 83: P. Wayre-NHP Agency; 84: L. Sirman; 85(above): Menatory; 86: Holmes-Lebel; 87: J. L. S. Dubois; 88: Okapia; 89 Lanceau-Jacana; 90: Buzzini; 91(above): Prenzel Press; 91(below): Treatt-Holmes-Lebel; 92: Martinerie-Fotogram; 93(above): Lanceau-Jacana; 93(below): F. Prenzel; 94(above): Fatras-Holmes-Lebel; 94(below): Buzzini; 95: Lanceau-Jacana; 96: Holmes-Lebel; 97: Buzzinin and Aarons; 98-9: Buzzini and Aarons; 100: F. Prenzel and Buzzini; 101(above): F. Prenzel and Buzzini; 101 below): Prenzel Press; 102(above): Buzzini; 102(below): Buzzini; 103: Buzzini; 104(both): Buzzini; 105: Prenzel Press; 106-7 (all): Buzzini; 108: Prenzel Press.

First published in this edition 1974

Published by William Collins Sons and Company Limited, Glasgow and London and by G. P. Putnam's Sons, New York

© 1968 Rizzoli Editore

© 1974 English language text William Collins Sons and Company Limited

Printed in Italy

ISBN 0 00 106108 9 (Collins)

SBN 399 11240 5 (G. P. Putnam's Sons)

Library of Congress Catalog Card Number: 73 85369

INTRODUCTION

Everybody knows what a cat looks like. It has been domesticated since ancient times, and is a typical mammal. It might well be selected as the prototype of the class Mammalia, which are the highest form of vertebrates and include man himself.

But, in addition, Felidae are the most typical representatives of one of the great orders of mammals—the Carnivora. The term "carnivorous", when used as an adjective, refers to any animal that eats other animals. For instance, sharks, birds of prey and many other species are carnivorous. It is equally correct to refer to plants like Venus's fly-trap as carnivorous. However, in zoology, for the most part, the term "carnivorous" is used to refer to a mammalian order (the carnivores) which, from a taxonomic point of view, is not at all easy to define.

It will help us in our study of the cats to place them within the total carnivorous context, so that we may have a better understanding of the way in which the zoologist classifies animals in the zoological system (animal taxonomy).

Today, carnivores form an extremely varied group, distributed throughout Eurasia, Africa and America, but not in Australia or the nearby islands.

Palaeontologically, they are the descendants of a primitive group of Creodontia, whose fossilized remains appear in the lower Paleocene (lower Tertiary strata) as small forms, similar to weasels (genus *Oxyclaenus*). Up to the Eocene period (upper or recent Tertiary), they underwent various modifications and then, at the end of this period, they disappeared.

The relationship between the extinct Creodontia and the Fissipedia (in other words the land carnivores) is not clear; But one of the most primitive groups (at the beginning of the Oligocene period) is that of the Felidae, some of whose fossils are really gigantic, like the "sabretoothed" or "dagger-toothed" tigers (fig. 1). The Pinnipedia, or aquatic carnivores (seal-type) appeared about the Miocene period.

Carnivores come in all different sizes. Side by side with small animals, such as cats, martens and stoats, are the very large animals like lions, the gray bear of the Rocky Mountains, the sea lions and the walruses. All of them are exceptional hunters or predators—in other words, beasts of prey. They hunt and kill other species (mice, deer, birds, fish, etc.). But their diet is not always, nor exclusively, made up of fresh meat, since many of them, like hyenas, eat carrion. Carrion is eaten by many other carnivores, including lions and tigers, when they are hungry or want a change of diet. Other carnivores, like the true bears, the 'washer' raccoons (*Procyon lotor*) and pandas (*Ailurus*) are virtually omnivorous. And there are some, like the badger, that are largely herbivorous.

The variations in the diet of carnivores are clearly reflected in the general appearance of the animals. The carnivores best adapted for hunting are the terrestrial ones (Fissipedia), whose limbs terminate in separate digits (fissiped means split foot), with strong, pointed nails or claws. The fissipeds are, therefore, "unguiculates". When they walk, some of them press the whole sole of the foot on the ground (plantigrade), some only part of it (semi-plantigrade), while others again walk on the tips of their toes (digitigrade) (fig. 2).

Plantigrade animals, like the bear, are typical walkers; digitigrade animals, such as the dog, are excellent runners and cats are very well adapted for speed and for leaping and bounding. This adaptation is most apparent in the retractile claws, which are operated by special ligaments and muscles, so that they can be withdrawn between special pads underneath the paws, avoiding becoming unnecessarily blunted. This can be clearly observed by studying the paw of a cat. The claws are unsheathed and extended when the cat pounces on its prey (fig. 3). Moreover, these special pads under the toes enable the cat to move soundlessly, an essential factor if it is to surprise its prey.

Aquatic carnivores, such as seals, have limbs with well-developed webbed feet, in the shape of fins, which is why they are called Pinnipedia (meaning 'finfooted').

Another characteristic of carnivores is the tendency for the big toe to be shorter on the front and back paws—many species do not even have one. The

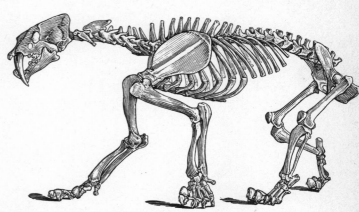

cat has five digits on its front feet and only four on the hind ones. The collar bones are very reduced or totally absent. The uterus of the female has two branches (bicornuate) and the number of offspring in a litter varies from one to more than a dozen. The number of pairs of mammary glands usually corresponds to the average size of litters. In Fissipedia, the young are born blind (as, for instance, kittens), whereas in Pinnipedia, their eyes are open and they are able to swim almost immediately after birth.

Apart from the above-mentioned points, the most distinctive characteristic of carnivores is revealed in their skeletons, especially the cranium and the teeth. The dentition in less developed forms has the primitive formula:

$$\frac{3}{3} \quad \frac{1}{1} \quad \frac{4}{4} \quad \frac{2}{3}$$

but in the cats this formula, and the corresponding dental structure, are considerably modified:

$$\frac{3}{3} \quad \frac{1}{1} \quad \frac{3}{2} \quad \frac{1}{1}$$

Of course, these different modifications depend upon the food they eat. The most noticeable characteristic of carnivores is the enormous development of the canines (as, for instance, in the lion and the dog). The last upper premolar and the first lower molar are known as the carnassials and, with their bevelled edges, act like shears.

Cats have prominent crests on the roof of the skull (occipital and pariental crests) for the insertion of the powerful masseter muscles that work the jaw.

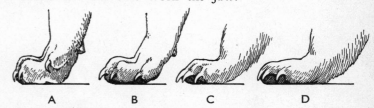

A   B   C   D

Figure 1: Complete restored skeleton of a [...] line of the pampas—Machairodus [...] (also called Smilodon necator or [...] lodon). The first fossils of this [...] line were discovered in Europe at the beginning of the nineteenth century. The Machairodus and Smilodon continued up to the Quaternary period.

Figure 2: Different ways of placing the foot on the ground in Fissipedia: A: digitigrade (dog, cat); B: semi-digitigrade (African civet); C: semi-plantigrade (Mustela); D: plantigrade (bear).

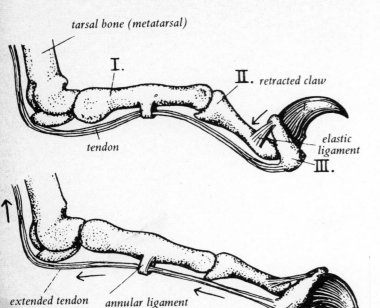

tarsal bone (metatarsal)

I.

II. retracted claw

tendon

elastic ligament

III.

extended tendon

annular ligament

extended claw III.

1

2

3

4

5

6

7

8

9

10

11

12

13

This characteristic is very marked in the lion's skull, and more so in that of male cats than in females.

Felines or Felidae, of which the common cat (genus *Felis*) is typical, are undoubtedly the most perfect examples of carnivores. Their perfectly formed, flexible, agile and muscular bodies act like well-oiled machines when they are leaping and hunting. Moreover, they are capable of climbing rocks and trees. Their eyesight ("lynx-eyed"), their cunning and patience, their graceful movements (noiseless thanks to the special pads beneath their paws), their quick reflexes, their sharp claws, their enormous carnassials and their powerful fangs—in short, all their special characteristics, make them formidable beasts of prey.

They normally prefer to hunt on their own and not in packs, and like to pursue their prey at full speed rather than lie in wait for it. They seize hold of their victim and half kill it with a well-aimed blow from their front paws, and then mortally wound it with a bite in the neck. The predator then feasts on the carcass, licking up the blood and then devouring the flesh. Cats tear the body to pieces with their carnassial teeth, which act like a sharp pair of scissors. The small mice and birds that are caught by cats are totally devoured; the big cats, however, devour only part of their prey. For example, a lion that has caught a large zebra or antelope will eat only the entrails and the muscular parts, but usually leaves most of the bones (thorax, backbone, etc.).

A typical feature of cats is their large whiskers, the hairs of which, long and stiff as bristles, act as tactile organs. They are called *vibrissae*. The rough tongue of the cats, covered with horny papillae, is another special characteristic. It is used to scrape off the flesh from the bones of their victims. Finally, their eyesight in twilight and darkness is very keen. In common with other animals that hunt at night, there is a reflecting layer behind the cat's retina—thus the eyeshine of the night hunter.

Of the hundreds of genera of Fissipedia existing today—more than two hundred species—about a fifth of them are cats. They live in all parts of the world, apart from the Antarctic, Australia, New Zealand, Madagascar,

Iceland and a few other islands.

Taxonomically, the most important genera are: *Felis*, which is typical of the whole group and from which the name of the family is derived. It contains the domestic and wild cats, the serval and nearly all the American felids; *Panthera* (including the big cats of the Old World —the lion, tiger and leopard, as well as the jaguar, also called the American tiger); *Lynx* (containing the common lynx, the caracal and others); and *Acinonyx* (which includes the cheetah or hunting leopard). The last genus consists of a group whose characteristics lie midway between the true felines and canids. The cheetah, for example, has non-retractile claws. It is a typical digitigrade animal, and very fast moving (it can run at up to sixty miles per hour).

The distinction between the genus *Felis* and that of *Panthera* made by George G. Simpson and other writers, but which is not accepted by some zoologists, is based mainly on the structure of the byoid bone and its ligaments which enable the big cats to roar, whereas in small and medium-sized cats the voice is limited to a characteristic miaowing.

The many species within each genus are usually divided in turn into subgenera, as, for example, *Felis concolor*, which is the puma; *Felis pardalis*, the ocelot; *Panthera uncia*, which is the snow leopard. There are also innumerable local breeds or genetic variations, especially within the group of domestic animals. The so-called black panthers are, in fact, darkly-hued varieties of the common leopard.

Figure 3: Toe of the hind paw of the cat. Above, with the claw retracted, and below, with claw extended. The matatarsus bone and the three phalanges (I, II, III) of the toe.

Figure 4: Different members of the Felidae family: 1) Ocelot (Leopardus pardalis); 2) Clouded Leopard (Panthera nebulosa); 3) Cheetah (Acinonyx jubatus); 4) Snow Leopard (Panthera uncia); 5) Puma (Felis concolor); 6) Jaguar (Panthera

8) Wildcat (Felis sylvestris); 9) Tige (Panthera tigris); 10) Ser neogoe (Leptailurus serval); 11) Felis sm leo); 12) Lynx (Lynx gigantic f cat (Octolobus man. related to the lynx.

CONTENTS

Carnivores
Fissipedia   12
Felidae   12
Cheetah   15
Panthera   22
Lion   22
Tiger   29
Leopard or Panther   50
Jaguar   63
Felis   69
Puma   69
Jaguarondi   71
Ocelot   73
Fisher Cat   74
Serval   75
European Wildcat   76
Gloved Cat   82
Lynx   83
Caracal   87
Domestic Cats   89

THE ORDER OF CARNIVORES

SUB-ORDER	Family	Sub-family	Genus
	Felidae		Acinonyx, Panthera, Felis, Lynx
	Hyaenidae	Hyaeninae	Hyaena, Crocuta
		Protelinae	Proteles
		Cryptoproctinae	Cryptoprocta
		Herpestinae	Xenogale, Cynictis, Rhynchogale, Bdeogale, Ichneumia, Crossarchus, Mungos, Atilax, Helogale, Herpestes, Suricata
	Viverridae	Galidinae	Salanoia, Mungotictis, Galidictis, Galidia
		Hemigalinae	Eupleres, Cynogale, Diplogale, Chrotogale, Hemigalus, Fossa
		Paradoxurinae	Arctictis, Macrogalidia, Paguma, Paradoxurus, Arctogalidia, Nandinia
		Viverrinae	Pardictis, Prionodon, Civettictis, Viverra, Osbornictis, Viverricula, Genetta, Poiana
FISSIPEDIA		Litrinae	Enhydra, Paraonyx, Aonyx, Amblonyx, Pteronura, Lutrogale, Lutra
		Mephitinae	Conepatus, Spilogale, Mephitis
	Mustelidae	Melinae	Melogale, Helictis, Taxidea, Mydaus, Arctonys, Meles
		Mellivorinae	Mellivora
		Mustelinae	Gulo, Poecilogale, Poecilictis, Zorilla, Lyncodon, Grisonella, Grison, Galera, Charronia, Martes, Vormela, Mustela
	Procyonidae	Ailurinae	Ailuropoda, Ailurus
		Procyoninae	Bassaricyon, Potos, Nasuella, Nasua, Procyon, Bassariscus
	Ursidae		Melursus, Helarctos, Thalarctos, Ursus, Selenarctos, Tremarctos
		Octocyoninae	Otocyon
	Canidae	Simocyoninae	Lycaon, Cuon, Speothos
		Caninae	Chrysocyon, Dusicyon, Nyctereutes, Urocyon, Fennecus, Vulpes, Alopex, Canis
		Cystophorinae	Mirounga, Cystophora
	Phocidae	Monachinae	Monachus
		Lobodontinae	Leptonychotes, Hydrurga, Ommatophoca, Lobodon
PINNIPEDIA		Phocinae	Erignathus, Halichoerus, Phoca
	Odobenidae		Odobenus
	Otariidae		Otaria, Eumetopias, Zalophus, Callorhinus, Arctocephalus

Carnivores are distributed over every continent of the world except Australia, the Antilles, a number of oceanic islands, New Zealand, and the Antarctic.

CARNIVORES

Carnivores are hunting animals that eat flesh. This is what the families in the order have in common; but they differ widely from each other in size, shape and style.

Land carnivores have well-developed limbs, perfectly designed for easy walking or running. The cheetah and the wolf are perfect examples.

The stomach of carnivores is a simple one, the intestine usually short and the caecum virtually non-existent. Nearly all carnivores possess anal glands, and these are especially well-developed in a family like the *Mustelidae*—the weasels. Anal glands are often called *stink glands* because their secretions smell strongly. There are several types of anal glands. Skunks have anal sacs that produce a foul-smelling liquid. In the *Viverridae*, the glands are really perfume sacs that secrete a fatty substance with a powerful

scent. In the badger and hyena there are sub-caudal glands—between the anus and the tail—that secrete a thick, fatty substance. Finally, there are the tubular glands surrounding the anus that are common to all the carnivores.

Carnivores, with their well-developed sense of smell, instantly know the scent of these anal secretions. The anal glands, in fact, play a vital role in the animals' actions. The secretions help them to contact each other and to recognize each other. The sexes identify each other in this way. The secretions are also used in marking territory, or for guiding the young—as in the case of badgers. Sometimes they are used even as a means of defence. The skunk, for example, can do more than stink—it can throw a stink-bomb at an enemy by squirting the secretion. Finally, the anal glands provide a fatty substance for oiling the skin.

The skull of the carnivores is elonga-

ted, with deep-set eye sockets, a prominent auditory duct and well-developed bone and cartilage of the nose. Such a conformation means plenty of room for the development of sight and hearing, both of which are vital to the animals of this order. The muzzle of the carnivores is more or less elongated, the nose hairless, the eyes large and alert and the ears erect. Bushy whiskers, or vibrissae, grow on the upper lip. These are tactile hairs—sensitive to touch. Thanks to very powerful muscles and sinews, the carnivores can all move with great agility, flexibility and speed.

All or some of the senses are acute. In some species the sense of smell is the best developed, while in others the most important is sight or hearing or touch. As a general rule carnivores are bold, patient and cunning.

Although by definition carnivores not all members of this order feed on meat alone. All of them obtain vegetable matter from the stomachs of their prey but some species eat a certain amount of vegetable matter—fruit, grain or grass. The latter are, therefore, omnivores rather than full-time carnivores. Bears and badgers are good examples of omnivorous carnivores. The dog, the fox and the pine marten are others. Nevertheless, such definitions can never be absolute because the omnivorous species always like meat when they can get it and prefer flesh to any other food.

In some of the carnivores, pairing is the rule, with the pairs staying together for some time after mating. Animals like foxes, some of the big cats and mustelids live together and help each other to feed and protect their young. But in the majority of species, the father tends to look on his own offspring as prey rather than as members of the family circle. The Scottish wildcat tom is like this. In such cases the mother is forced to hide her young and she will drive away her mate if he discovers their hiding place.

Litter size varies considerably from species to species and from family to family. One young is unusual although it occurs in the seals. The young are nearly always born with their eyes closed and all of them are helpless at birth. But the period of helplessness varies. In some species it is very short, in others it is prolonged. Development

The genet is an African member of the Viverridae family, distinguished by the many dark markings on its skin and by its long annulated tail.

then proceeds rapidly. The mother protects her young and stays with them until they can fend for themselves. Females of many species will carry off their offspring at any threat of danger. The majority carry their young as a cat carries kittens. Some carry them on their backs or between their forelegs.

The holding of territory is a common part of the pattern of carnivores; but they do not all behave in the same way. Territoriality can be said to fall roughly into two categories. First of all there is the type of area in which many members of a species live, and which is cut up into individual territories criss-crossed by pathways. All the animals of that species in the area can use these pathways without hindrance or fear of hostile display from others of their own kind. This is true, for example, in the case of paths leading to waterholes. Such paths are no man's land or anybody's. Within this general area, the individual or family territory is marked out.

Animals living in a community do not adhere so strictly to individual territories. But in the case of animals like weasels and stoats, each territory is usually guarded jealously against all intruders of the same species. It is not actively guarded against animals of other species unless there is some form of direct competition. The holder of a

territory defends it by aggressive display; this posturing is usually enough to keep a competitor out. A real fight takes place only when the owner of the territory is weaker than the intruder. If he is stronger the intruder is driven off and pursued to the territorial limit—not beyond it.

Carnivores, like many other animals, mark out their territories in three ways—by setting scent, by display, or by sound. Scent is set by secretions from the glands which have already been mentioned. Urine is also used to mark territory—as it is by dogs. And, of course, the voice is used. Lions roar, foxes yap and wolves howl.

Within the animal's territory is its lair or den or nest and, within this zone, no other animal is allowed to hunt or to intrude. Well-trodden paths lead from this zone, and the animal uses them at all times when leaving its den. This

(Above)
The "washer" raccoon is a carnivore with non-rectractile claws. It has a bushy tail marked with rings of dark hair. It is to be found only in the New World.

(Top)
The ermine (or stoat) is a member of the Mustelidae family, which lives in the northern hemisphere. The summer coat is brown, but it sheds it in the late autumn and becomes white (ermine) in winter. Its tail tip

fact is well known and used by hunters.

To sum up: the order of carnivores contains species showing the following characteristics: A diet of flesh or fish, although some species are omnivorous.

A dentition varying considerably according to the family, but which usually consists of forty-two teeth, arranged as follows for each side of the upper and lower jaws respectively: incisors 3/3, canines 1/1, premolars 4/4, molars 2/3. The canine teeth are nearly always powerful and very prominent, taking the form of fangs.

A brain with well-developed hemispheres.

A rudimentary or non-existent collarbone.

Offspring that are born helpless, with closed eyes, hairless and incapable of walking.

The order of carnivores, which has a very wide geographical distribution, is divided into two sub-orders: the *Fissipedia* that walk on land; and the *Pinnipedia*—animals with fins instead of feet, adapted to living in the water.

FISSIPEDIA

This sub-order contains all the carnivores with feet. The feet have four or five toes. *Fissipedia* are either plantigrade, which means that they place the whole sole of the foot on the ground when they are walking (as the bear does) or they are digitigrade, which means they place only the tip of the toes on the ground (as the lion does). The eyes of the fissipeds have a layer of special cells that cause them to shine in the dark (eyeshine). Fissipeds are carnivorous, and their stomach is very simple. The sub-order is divided into seven families: *Felidae, Hyaenidae, Viverridae, Mustelidae, Procyonidae, Ursidae* and *Canidae*.

FELIDAE

This is the family of the cats. Of all the carnivores, the cats are the most perfectly developed, the most numerous and, in many ways, the most important. They are all hunters and flesh-eaters and vary in size from the very big (like the tiger) to the very small (like the domestic cat). They are robust and elegant in form with a flexible spinal column that adds to their grace of movement. They are agile and dexterous, able to leap and bound with great speed.

The head of the cat is round, supported on a sturdy neck. The ears are small.

The eyes are large, with round or almond-shaped pupils that dilate in the dark when the animals are over-excited. The effect of bright light on the pupil is the reverse; it contracts until it is no more than a narrow vertical slit. Cats

12

The coyote is an omnivorous canine, but is predominantly carnivorous. Smaller than the wolf, it lives in pairs and hunts in bands. It is the jackal of the New World.

eyesight is not very good at a distance, but it becomes more acute when their field of vision is reduced. The muzzle is usually flattened in contrast to that of the dog. On each side of the upper jaw there are three incisors, one canine, three premolars and one molar. The canine teeth are long, thick, sharp and slightly hooked, protruding well beyond the other teeth. The prominent canines hide the incisors and make the molars look harmless by comparison although, in actual fact, they too are strong and sharp. With such teeth, generally grooved and sharp-edged, the cat is well equipped to wound, lacerate and tear prey to pieces.

Cats' tails are usually fairly long—an exception being the European wildcat whose tail is clubbed. The front paws have five digits; the hind paws only four. All these toes have curved, pointed nails known as claws, which are powerful weapons. When the cat is walking, the claws are withdrawn into sheaths so that they do not become blunted.

On the sole of its foot, the cat has fleshy, elastic pads sometimes covered with thick hairs. These pads cushion the foot, enabling the cat to walk noiselessly.

The fur of cats is usually thick and soft. Hue varies with species and can be plain as in pumas, spotted as in leopards, or striped as in tigers.

Cats' hearing is their most acute sense. They can hear the faintest of

sounds from some distance away, even when the prey animal is walking on sand. This faculty is vital when the cat is hunting, and compensates for its poor eyesight.

The cat's whiskers, or vibrissae, are tactile organs—organs of touch. The hair over the eyes perform the same function. In the lynx, there are tufts of hair on the ears that are equally sensitive. Indeed, the whole of the cat's body has great tactile sensitivity.

Cats have a delicate sense of taste. They prefer food that is only slightly salty or sweetish and are fond of liquids of animal origin, such as milk and blood.

Cats are found in America and in the Old World, apart from Madagascar. They are not found in Australia. They occur in many types of habitat—plains, mountains, dry sandy regions as well as humid, low-altitude areas; wooded country as well as grasslands. Forests provide them with the kind of cover they need. They can den up there or retreat when pursued by enemies. In such cover they can lie in wait and pounce on their prey without warning. In general, cats do not have permanent dens. They are active mainly from dusk to dawn, but many cats will lie up during the night if conditions are not right or if they are under pressure from man. If surprised by an enemy when out hunting, they will retire into the first hiding place they come across.

All cats are good swimmers and they all hunt their prey in much the same way. They will stalk prey or lie up and take it from ambush. They hunt carefully, without noise, their ears sensitive to the slightest sound. When they cannot see a prey they will use their ears or their noses to track it down. They are proverbially patient and will wait for hours on end until a prey species comes to them. Then they attack from ambush. The cat's final approach to a prey is a creeping stalk on the leeward side, closing in with a single bound or a series of bounds, for the pounce. The claws are holding weapons; the teeth are the killers. The cat usually bites the neck of its victim, or the flank, and it holds on until the prey is dead.

Pallas's cat or the Steppes cat lives in Asia and preys on small rodents. Its very bushy fur has dark, transverse stripes.

(Top)
Cats are found all over the world except in Madagascar and Australia.

13

Although cats can move at great speed, their powers of endurance are limited and they will attack only animals that they can be sure of killing at the first strike—or of grounding. They will seldom pursue an animal which they have wounded but failed to kill. Once a cat has made its kill, it drags the dead animal to a secluded spot where it can be devoured under cover. But sometimes the cat will eat on the spot. When prey is abundant the cat will often kill more than it needs, eating only the choicest parts and leaving the rest. Cats thus share their prey with other carnivores, the others taking what the cat does not want. The big cats attack man only in rare circumstances, or when an old or wounded animal, unable to hunt normal prey, finds him an easy victim. Many man-eaters have been made like this by man, in the sense that they have been disabled by gunshot or other means.

Female cats have four nipples on the stomach and sometimes four more on the chest. They usually have several young at a birth. A litter of one is rare. The cat devotes much time to her kittens, teaching them cleanliness first of all. When she has young, the female cat can become extremely aggressive, defending her young against all attacks, even when her own life is at stake. In many species, the female has to protect her offspring against attacks from their own father. Tom-cats are liable to eat their own family, especially when the kittens' eyes are still closed. Quite often the female cat offers her young small animals, either living or dead, so that they can learn how to tear up a carcass. When they are still very young, she will take them on hunting trips and they learn by her example. When the kittens are old enough to fend for themselves, they leave the family and, for some time, live a solitary existence, wandering around until they can find a territory of their own.

All of the cats are stalkers except the cheetah which courses game like a greyhound.

Cats are active usually at night.

The Felidae family, which is found over practically the whole area occupied by the order of the CARNIVORA, consists of four genera in a total of thirty-six species. The genera are: *Acinonyx*, *Panthera*, *Felis* and *Lynx*.

14

(Top)
The leopard cat is a small feline which hunts at night and takes refuge, during the daytime, in hollows of trees.

(Above)
The tiger is a very large cat. Its structure resembles that of the lion. Its striped coat is like that of no other cat. It is very difficult to capture, but adapts _____ to captivity.

Cheetah

The cheetah or "hunting leopard" (*Acinonyx jubatus*) is sometimes called the cat dog, and this is not surprising because in many ways it resembles the dog more closely than it does other cats. The spotted coat, round head and long tail are cat; the remainder of the body is dog. Like the dogs it has long, slim legs and non-retractile claws. As a result, its claws become as readily blunted as the nails of dogs. They are not at all adapted to gripping prey but they are well adapted for running. However, despite its likeness to a large, spotted greyhound, the cheetah is in no way related to the dog family. Its appearance is the result of convergent evolution. Two unrelated species become like each other because they lead the same kind of lives, shaped by similar pressures. Thus the whale is fish-like, and the swift superficially resembles the unrelated swallow. Nevertheless the cheetah shows another remarkable similarity to the dog—it can be tamed and trained and, in fact, often is.

It is a slim, agile animal with much longer legs than other cats. It has a very small head with a rather elongated muzzle. Its ears are small and set widely apart. In its eyes, it again resembles the dog because the pupils are round. Its fur is smooth, slightly shaggy in parts, especially on the back, and varies in hue. The under-fur is usually a very beautiful pale yellow. The markings are black and brown, round in shape and set very closely together. These spots, which almost merge on the back, form rings on the tail. The cheetah can reach a length of five feet plus its tail of two and a half feet. It is a tall cat and may stand as tall as three feet at the shoulder. It has a neck mane of varying length. At one

(Top)
The cheetah is a cat superbly adapted for swift running: it is long-limbed and has non-retractile claws, a long, muscular tail and a small head. It is the swiftest of all mammals.

(Above)
Cheetahs often hunt in pairs, one of them running down the prey and the other attacking the animal, whose resistance has been broken down by the chase.

time the cheetah was much more common and more widely distributed than it is today. It was found from India to Arabia, including Western Asia and Africa. Now it is extremely rare in India and becoming progressively rarer in Africa.

Ruminants of small or medium size are the cheetah's main prey. Antelopes are the first choice of any prey species so the cheetah is most likely to be found in areas where these animals are plentiful. It runs them down, coursing them as a greyhound courses a hare.

Various tests have shown that the cheetah is the fastest of all land mammals. It has great speed—up to 79 miles per hour according to some reckonings—so has no difficulty in getting out of the way of its slower moving enemies. As a result it has little need of cover, so is not found in the forest depths. Usually it dens up in a rock cleft in the lowest hills.

When the hunting cheetah views a grazing herd of antelopes or gazelles it begins to crawl stealthily towards them. It is an expert stalker, and moves with great stealth, so it rarely alarms such flighty, nervous game. The cheetah always stalks in from the leeward side. Every time the leader of the herd raises

16

(Top)
The gestation period of the cheetah lasts from 84 to 95 days, and the female gives birth to two to four offspring. The mother takes great care of them and becomes very dangerous if anyone tries to get near them.

(Above)
The cheetah is the most docile of the cats. It can be domesticated and trained for hunting. In captivity, however, it becomes delicate, fears the cold and does not thrive for long in a cage that is too narrow.

(Right)
The lions of southern Africa join together in bands to hunt. They often climb up into trees to inspect their hunting territory.

This cheetah with its young
is not interested in the
stationary gnus.
When a big cat passes a group
of herbivores, the latter know
if there is any danger.

its head to look round, the cheetah freezes and remains motionless. It stays still until the head goes down again. The cheetah continues its stalk, moving in when all the heads are down and freezing the moment one goes up. By the time it is within striking distance, the cheetah knows which animal it is going to attack. The attack is a rush and a pounce without warning.

In Nairobi Park, Kenya, a family of cheetahs was observed hunting in company with a band of jackals. The jackals were acting as decoys, attracting the attention of the quarry while the cheetahs moved in. Cheetahs and jackals had obviously discovered it was to their mutual advantage to work in this way.

Although it can attain such high speeds over a short distance, the cheetah lacks endurance; in fact, it can be run down and overtaken by a good horse. Besides being a remarkable runner, it is a considerable high jumper. When bounding, it can leap nine feet into the air. However, unlike the other cats, it cannot climb trees.

The gestation period in the cheetah is about 90 days, and two litters a year are usual. The number of young born varies from two to four.

Man has long exploited the cunning and the exceptional speed of the cheetah by taming it and using it on his own hunting expeditions in the same way as he uses the greyhound. The animals were much used in India during big hunts. They used to be used in Europe too; also in Mongolia.

Young cheetahs cannot be trained to hunt with man. In India only adult animals are used, but they must be allowed great freedom of action, and are only entrusted to very experienced hunters.

No member of the cat family is more docile than the cheetah. If it is tethered it makes no attempt to bite through the rope with its teeth, or to break it by kicking. It never attacks those who take care of it and can be approached and stroked without danger. It will remain motionless for hours at a time, staring into space and purring as though it were day-dreaming. At such times, chickens, goats and sheep can come within striking distance of it without risk, for it takes no notice of them.

Cheetahs kept in zoos are easily

(Left)
Lion cubs are squat and clumsy. They play and miaow like cats, which they resemble. Their movements are slow and awkward.

When attacking a herd of antelopes, the cheetah crawls along the ground silently and to the leeward side. It springs with a single bound upon its prey, which it eats on the spot.

managed and fed, but they are more delicate than other cats of similar size. They cannot survive in small cages and suffer much more from cold than do lions or tigers. When a female cheetah gives birth to a family in captivity she usually refuses to feed them and they have to be artificially reared.

Panthera

These large cats are distinguished from the genus *Felis* by the suspensory apparatus of the hyoid bone which is imperfectly ossified and allows for great mobility of the larynx.

We shall be studying in turn the lion, the tiger and the leopard or panther.

Lion

Since time immemorial the lion has been known as the king of beasts and one needs merely to look at him to understand why. He is big, powerful and heavily maned. Yet he is neither the largest of the cat family, nor the strongest or swiftest; but he is certainly the biggest carnivore in Africa and the most impressive.

The lion (*Panthera leo*, formerly known as *Felis leo*) is easily distinguished from all other cats.

He has a robust body with the powerful limbs typical of the carnivores. He is massive in front and broad-chested, but his hind quarters are narrow, with tucked-up belly and lean flanks. He has a very large head, almost rectangular in shape, a broad, rounded snout and wide, flared ears. His eyes are medium-sized with round, yellow pupils. His legs are stronger than those of any other cat. His long tail ends in a horny tip with a tuft of hair.

The lion's coat is smooth, close-laid, glossy and bright—reddish-yellow or tawny-brown. Many of the lion's body hairs are black-tipped or totally black, giving the effect of changing hues which is typical of this cat. In the male, the head and neck is covered by a thick, bushy mane, consisting of long, smooth hair that hangs down in front as far as the top of the forelegs, half-way across the back and down the sides. Part of the forelimbs is covered with hair longer

Since the cheetah is the swiftest of all mammals, it does not need to hide itself in the depths of impenetrable forests. It can elude its enemies with a few leaps.

The lion has robust and powerful limbs. Its
paws are stronger than those of other felines. Its
tail terminates in a horny point, decorated with
a tuft of hairs. Its broad snout   ed by
an opulent mane.

birth coat is grayish woolly hair. The lioness has a plain coat, like her cubs. She is smaller than the male and does not have a mane, although she has longer hair on the fore part of her body than on the hind.

Many centuries ago the Romans collected hundreds of lions for their arenas and used them in their brutal circuses at Rome. Nowadays, it would be impossible to collect lions in such numbers. Herodotus tells us that when Xerxes's army was passing through Macedonia, a group of lions attacked the camel train in the dark. The soldiers, unaware that such animals existed in the country, were amazed to see them. Aristotle reports that the lion did not exist in any other part of Europe. It is impossible now to establish the precise period when the lion died out in Europe, but it must certainly have been over a thousand years ago. The Bible tells us that, in ancient times, the lion was also found in Syria and Palestine. But here again there is no exact information as to when it disappeared from the Holy Land. All we know is that the lion formerly existed in an area stretching from the Cape of Good Hope to North Africa, and to Southern Asia as far as India.

Today, the lion's range is much more restricted. Not only has it disappeared from North Africa, where it was still plentiful in the nineteenth century; it has also disappeared from the Cape.

In the rest of Africa, its numbers vary from one region to another. It is still found in the Sudan, Kenya, Tanzania and West Africa as far as the Congo. It is also found in a large part of West Africa south of the Sahara, as far as Senegal and Gambia. There are still lions in Chad, in the Central African Republic and, from this area, they spread to central-southern Africa, except the extreme south. The lion, in fact, is declining rapidly in competition with man. It is found nowadays only on the plains and savannas and in mountainous areas where there is an abundance of game.

Lions are extinct in Iran and Iraq, although the Persian lion *(Panthera Leo persica)*, which is a distinct sub-species, can still be found in the Gir forest in the Kathiawar region of India. These are the only lions left in India. It is not true, therefore, to say that there are no lions in India.

In North Africa each lion occupies a clearly defined territory and seldom has cause to fight other lions when he is out searching for food. If he does become involved in combat with another lion

than that on the rest of the body. The mane is tawny-yellow, flecked with reddish-black on the head and neck. Some male lions have no manes, just as some stags have no antlers.

A fully grown adult male lion will stand from two and a half to three feet tall at the shoulder. Body length is from five to eight feet plus two to three feet of tail. Yet the lion cub at birth measures just over a foot in length, which is about the size of an adult domestic cat. The

(Top)
The lion's distribution in Africa, south of the Sahara, is very irregular. It exists in India, in the Gir forest, where the last of the Asiatic lions—formerly plentiful in western Asia— are protected from extinction.

(Above)
The lion still lives in the African savanna. It likes to roam the steppes and mountainous or grassy regions where herbivores graze. These are its main prey.

it is usually during the mating season.

In South Africa, on the other hand, lions gather together in bands for the purpose of hunting. At the end of the dry season, from May to September, great herds of antelopes and large numbers of zebras abandon the dried-up plains and migrate in search of better grasslands. At journey's end, they herd together in great numbers on the new pastures. The lions, moving in bands, follow the migrating herds throughout their long journey and right into their new grazing grounds.

Lions are rarely found in closed forest. They prefer open ground—grassy plains scattered with bushes; scattered woodland or small clumps of trees in which they can find shade during the daytime; arid steppes and other deserted and isolated regions where their tawny coats serve as camouflage. They like sheltered spots to den up in but, during the migra-

tory period, they pick the first place they can find just before dawn.

In general the lion resembles the other big cats. Like any other predator, prey is his first consideration and he takes the shortest route to this, picking the easiest and most available victims. So, in the eastern Sudan, he follows the migratory herds, day after day, week after week, picking out the weaklings, the old, the aged, and the diseased. Because he is mainly nocturnal in habits he is not often seen during the day, but he will come out before nightfall when he has to. In the daytime, he will be found in scrub areas where the scrub provides both shade and cover. The lion in settled territory parades his perimeter like any other territory-holding mammal, usually picking a high point from which to view his frontiers.

Everybody has heard of the lion's roar but those who have heard it are

relatively few. It is the same with the howling of wolves. There are people who have lived in wolf country all their lives who have never heard a wolf call, and people who have lived among lions all their lives who have never heard a lion roar. Like the sounds uttered by any other mammals, the roar of the lion has meaning. It is a contact signal between the sexes or an expression of satisfaction after a heavy meal. The roar, once heard, is never likely to be confused with a sound uttered by any other animal. Yet it is difficult to describe. It has been described as the miaow of a cat amplified many times and distorted; but, in fact, other ears do not hear it in this way. It is a deep bass, chesty roar. The Arabs describe it with an expressive word *raad* which means thunder, and this is possibly the best way of describing it—a thunderous growl.

The lion's roar starts in the depths of

Lions hunt at night or at dusk, near waterholes where the herds go to drink water. The lion prefers large game to small and also eats carrion. But it rarely attacks man.

25

the chest, causing the walls to vibrate. It is uttered with the head held low toward the ground and this posture helps in producing the roar. When the lion is afraid he utters a long, continuous cry, laying his ears back and sweeping the ground with his tail.

The lion's roar has meaning for other lions. Its effect on other predators has not been studied but can be extraordinary. When a hyena hears a lion roaring it stops howling. The leopard stops growling. Both listen to the so-called king of beasts. Monkeys, on the other hand, begin to leap frantically up and down and climb to the highest branches of the trees, intensifying their cries as they do so. Herds of antelopes flee from the sound. Herds of cattle stop calling. Even a well-trained camel, used to carrying loads and to being ordered about by man, suddenly begins to tremble and refuses to obey its master. It is liable to toss off its load and take flight. A horse will rear and back away from the sound. The domestic dog will run from the house or from its master, howling. Human beings find the roar impressive and many people are afraid when they first hear it. In East Africa, villagers will not walk on the roads after dark when there are lions about.

In North Africa lions are often found close to villages, where they can become a nuisance by raiding domestic livestock, especially goats. David Livingstone has recorded that "When the lion is too old to go hunting for game, he enters the village in search of goats. But if by any chance he encounters a woman or a child, he seizes them without much ado." This statement requires a great deal of qualification. A very old lion, unable to hunt normal game, is liable to become a man-eater. But the man-eating lion is exceptional. A lion that has been wounded by gunshot may become a man-eater. From time to time there are lions that become man-eaters because, living close to human habitations, they have lost this fear of man. An old or weak lion soon learns that man is an easy prey.

Game herds show little concern in the presence of a lion or lionesses that are not hunting, but once the lions begin to hunt, the herds take action, beginning to move, at first leisurely, and then in

(Top)
In order to obtain its food more easily, the lion follows the nomadic herds and lies in wait for the prey it intends to kill. It often hunts with a companion—antelopes, giraffes, zebras and buffalo.

(Above)
When lion cubs are born, they weigh over two pounds. They are born in a specially prepared bed, situated deep in dense bushes and close to a waterhole.

panic. The lions take the outliers and the weak animals and as soon as a kill is made the other animals in the herd stop running away and return to their grazing or their resting. A herd, in fact, will stand still when lions are parading along their flank.

In East Africa, much research has recently been done on lions. Brian Bertram of Cambridge has been fitting collars with built-in radio transmitters on the leading lions in a number of prides. By this method, he can "home in" on the prides at any time, night or day, and study their actions and structure. It is only rarely that all the lions in a pride are together at the same time.

They are social animals, much more so than any other cat. The social unit is made up of several lionesses, with a leading male and subordinate males. There may be as many as 17 animals in such a unit. The lionesses in the pride do the hunting and the killing. Once a kill has been made, the male feeds first. When he has eaten all he can hold, the lionesses take their turn. There is thus a high mortality rate among cubs that have been weaned. If the lions are killing big prey there is enough left for the cubs. If prey is small and lion and lionesses devour it all, the cubs go without. There is no question of the weaned cubs being fed first. Sometimes an intruding lion will drive off the territorial lioness or lionesses and steal the prey. The territorial lion, if he is within striking distance, will chase the intruder and recover the prey.

The lioness gives birth to her young 15 or 16 weeks after mating. The litter usually consists of two or three cubs but there may be up to six. At birth the cubs are the size of a domestic cat and weigh a little over two pounds. They are born with their eyes wide open, which is exceptional.

The lioness usually selects a den in a thicket near a waterhole or river. In this way she can catch game without having to go too far from her cubs. She attends to her cubs with great care. Lion cubs at birth are fat, squat and spotted. They learn to walk at about the age of two months. After that they begin to play with each other like domestic kittens. At first they miaow like cats. Later on voices become fuller and stronger. they are six months old, they are

After every meal, lions go and drink water. Their prey know that at such times there is nothing to fear from them, and do not run away.

27

able to follow their mother for short distances when she goes hunting. They are weaned about this time. By the end of a year, they are about the size of a large dog. The sexes are still very much alike, but the differences soon begin to show. The young males are stronger and more thick-set. At the age of three their manes begin to show. Male and female are fully developed by the age of six or seven years. The life span of the lion is directly related to this slow rate of development. Lions in captivity have been known to live for about 17 years.

Lions hunt game animals at water-holes. In the semi-arid areas, where both live, the distance between drinking places can be very great, so the animals travel to drink in troupes and herds. Lions will lie in wait or stalk into animals that are drinking. The stalking lion comes from the leeward, so that the drinking animals cannot get his scent on the wind; then he makes his attack. Game animals approaching the water-hole come in downwind so that they can smell any lion in ambush. The animal that comes in upwind with the lion lying below is liable to be killed because it has broken the rules of safety, as it were.

Every predator has its prey range and the lion is no exception. His prey range is from the very small, like grasshoppers, to the very large, like wildebeests and zebras. On the whole, he prefers animals on the big side but, in an emergency, he can stay alive and satisfy his hunger on very small creatures. Bigger prey includes zebras, buffalo, impala, wilde-

beests, warthogs and animals of similar size. No lion would dream of attacking an elephant or a rhinoceros, as either could kill him.

Because he preys upon the grazing animals of the African savannas, the lion is an important unit in the ecological equilibrium of these areas. By preying upon ungulates, he helps maintain an overall balance. Although the lion prefers to eat prey that he has killed himself, he will attack animals that are put out as baits by hunters—for example the goat. Under certain circumstances he will eat carrion, even carrion in an advanced state of decomposition. A dead elephant, even if it is crawling with maggots, will not be their the lion cannot find fresh pr Whc return to it night after n

28

The lion only hunts when it is hungry. The other animals know when it is replete and, while remaining at a safe distance, go on grazing and drinking without fear.

Tiger

Although the lion is known as the king of beasts, it is not the biggest cat. Some lions are bigger than some tigers, but the tigers are the biggest of the cats. A really big tiger of the Siberian race may weigh up to 650 pounds and measure over 13 feet from the tip of its nose to the tip of its tail. Other races are smaller and it would be true to say that there are many more tigers of about nine feet in length than there are over that size. The average weight is between 400 and 500 pounds and such an animal would stand about three feet tall at the shoulder. Tigresses are smaller than tigers and around four fifths of their weight.

Several races of tiger exist, which is

(Top)
The tiger has a rounded head, well proportioned to its body. It has a short, shaggy beard on each side of its snout. The pupil of the eye is round and yellowish. Its incisors are brownish.

(Above)
The tiger is to be found throughout Asia from Siberia, in the north, as far as Java, in the south. It is not found in Tibet, Ceylon or Borneo.

30   *The tiger is a huge, striped cat. The background of its coat is dark yellow on the back and becomes lighter toward the flanks. Dark, transverse stripes, curving inward toward the back, make an irregular pattern on its coat.*

not surprising considering the animal's wide distribution and the variety of habitats it occupies. Its range in Asia is greater than the area of Europe—from latitude 8° south to 55° north, into south-east Siberia. It is found in the largest numbers in the hot areas of Asia and East India. It ranges from northern India eastward to Amur and into China. In the west it ranges through Iran and Afghanistan to the shores of the Caspian Sea. In the south it is found in India, Burma, Malaysia, Sumatra, Java and Bali. It is not found in Ceylon, Tibet or Borneo.

Throughout this wide range the tiger varies widely in size, markings and density of coat. The coat varies from yellow to orange-red, and may even be white. The fur is palest on the throat, belly and the inside of the legs. The well-known stripes can be black or dark brown. The stripes are vertical on the body and horizontal on the legs. The face striping is variable and may form whorls, loops or spots.

The biggest race is that found in Siberia, and is known as the Siberian or Amur tiger. It is not so vivid as the tropical races, its coat being pale yellow-ish in winter and only slightly redder in summer; but it is notable for its very long and thick winter coat and its heavily furred, shaggy tail. This race is protected by law. It was once under threat of extinction, and a census carried out in the 1960s suggested that its numbers were down to about 100 in the whole of Manchuria and Siberia. Today, tigers are protected over most of their range.

The Royal Bengal tiger is smaller than the Siberian race; but only slightly so. This is a variegated tiger with short fur and a tapering tail. The facial mark-ings of the Bengal tiger are white flashes ringed with black. This race is found from the Himalayas to southern India.

The Caspian tiger has longer and thicker hair than the Bengal tiger and the stripes on its flanks are dark brown instead of black. The smallest race is the Sumatran tiger, which is found only on the island of Sumatra. It is the smallest of the tigers, deep orange with broad black striping.

When Blake wrote "Tyger, tyger, burning bright" he was thinking of the animal out of its natural habitat—as in fact one sees the animal in zoos—vivid with highly contrasting stripes. Yet in its forest habitat the coat is neither bright nor burning. It helps the tiger to blend with its background of sunlight and barred and dappled shadows—in the jungle, or among grasses and tawny reeds. When it is running through the forest it looks gray even at close range. The tiger is further adapted to a forest life by having flattened flanks so that it can squeeze easily between bushes and trees.

Tigers are, in the main, nocturnal

In the luxuriant jungle, where the sun filters through the vegetation, the tiger's coat blends with its background to such an extent that it becomes invisible, even to the eyes of the most suspicious of its prey.

31

animals. This is especially so where they are under much pressure from man or even where there is much disturbance of the habitat by man. But in quieter areas they will hunt by day. In the jungles of Malaya they are notable for being active during daylight. When hunting by day they like to avoid direct sunlight. As a general rule, however, the tiger, throughout its range, becomes active mainly after sunset.

Tigers prey mainly on wild pigs, deer and antelopes but their prey range is wide—from the very small to the very large. Analysis of the stomachs of wild tigers has shown that they even eat frogs, mice and insects. Other prey items are turtles, fish, locusts, monkeys and porcupines. The tiger will not attack either elephants or buffalo, but it will kill their young. Domestic live-stock are often killed, but the tiger favours wild game and has been known to desert an area with plenty of cattle but no wild game.

The tiger is a specialist predator on wild pigs, which cause tremendous damage to young forests by rooting in the ground. The importance of the tiger's predation on this species is now generally recognized.

Although tigers eat porcupines, these can be a dangerous prey because the quills can cause serious injury and it is a fact that a tiger so injured may become a man-eater as a result.

Like most other wild animals, the tiger normally avoids man; but a wounded tiger will counter-attack, charging blindly into a group of hunters. A spear is a poor weapon against such a counter-attack; even a rifle is not much good unless in experienced hands. Five or six hundredweights of wounded tiger striking a man and ripping with claws and teeth usually has only one result—the man is crippled or dies.

But it is unlikely that the tiger will eat him. Some tigers eat many people; most tigers do not eat anybody. Most tigers do not kill humans. Yet one hears much about the tiger as a man-eater.

The late Jim Corbett, one of the great experts on tigers and a man with an unbounded admiration for them, knew more about man-eaters than anyone before or since. Corbett produced much evidence to show that man-eaters were, more often than not, man-made. A

In spite of its large size, the tiger moves with great suppleness and lightness. It moves silently, flattening itself against the ground when it is on the look-out for prey.

tiger suffering from wounds caused by bullets or spears became unfit to hunt his usual prey and turned to the easiest one—man.

Despite their rarity, however, man-eaters take a heavy toll. In the Madhja Pradesh district of India, a man-eater killed 52 people within three months in 1960. Jim Corbett, because of, rather than in spite of, his admiration for tigers, specialized in shooting man-eaters. He shot the notorious man-eating tigress of Champawat, in the sub-Himalayan Kumoan, which had killed 434 people.

A man-eating tiger or tigress of this kind can threaten a large vicinity. The animal completely loses its fear of man and will approach, and even enter, human dwellings in the middle of the day. Jim Corbett has recorded the case of a man who actually escaped from a man-eater. Corbett recorded:

"A really remarkable case in which a man attacked by a tiger succeeded in saving his life at the last moment occurred in the sub-Himalayan Kumoan. A native was cutting grass above a steep slope and just when he was tying up the grass he was attacked by the tiger which was known through the region as the Chowgarh man-eater. The tiger got hold of the man's head with its jaws. One of its fangs penetrated his cheek under the eye; one canine penetrated his chin; and the remaining two penetrated his neck where it joins the back. With its great weight the tiger bore the man to the ground. Fortunately he did not lose consciousness. Chest to chest, man and tiger lay on the edge of the steep slope. However, when falling to the ground, the man had managed to get hold of a small tree and his arms and legs were still free. As all cats do, the tiger held its victim for a while after the attack. In spite of the terrible pain, the Indian slowly drew up his legs and pushed violently against the tiger's belly. In this way he succeeded in pushing the tiger over the edge of the slope and so saved his life. The tiger fell down the slope and did not come back. The severely wounded man bandaged his head with his loin cloth and succeeded in reaching his village. When he was well again only his terribly disfigured head bore witness to the fact that he had come so close to death."

Another man-eater, a tigress known

The tiger usually makes its lair along the river banks among the rushes and the bamboo thickets. It lives in its chosen lair, however rudimentary it may be, for many years— either alone, or in small groups.

The pattern of stripes decorating the head of certain tigers might evoke a character in Chinese writing of sacred significance. Such tigers would then become the object of worship.

35

as the "Tiger of Benchipur", lived in Mysore around 1870. The inhabitants of 13 villages were forced to abandon their homes, and the harvest over an area of 300 square miles was endangered as a result. For a long time she evaded all attempts to destroy her but was finally killed by Corbett. Between 1877 and 1886, nearly 1,000 people were killed each year in India by man-eaters. During this same period up to 2,000 tigers were killed annually.

A famous tiger hunter called Forsythe made a point often made by Corbett—that a man-eater is extremely difficult to locate unless one is prepared to have infinite patience.

He wrote:

"Well I can assure you that there is no danger in travelling through the wild regions of India frequented by a man-eating tiger. But to allay the fears of impressionable people I would like to add that I have never yet had a tiger attack any camp I set up even although I was not always surrounded by all the necessary precautions. Those who do not know these parts are always astonished to see the experienced hunter leave his tent and lie down peacefully outside under the stars to listen, before going to sleep, to the voices of the animals."

Apart from man, the tiger appears to have only one enemy—a small dog-like Indian carnivore about 20 inches tall and three feet in length. It has been reported that this animal, which hunts in packs, can run a tiger to death, biting pieces out of it until it succumbs from loss of blood. But there is no concrete evidence for this story and it may be untrue.

The tiger loves water, bathes regularly and is an excellent swimmer. Whether he lives in thick forest, open forest or plantations, he usually has his lair near a river bank or among reeds and bamboo thickets. He likes solitude, lush vegetation, and waterholes where he can bathe and quench his thirst. He is a territorial animal and once he has established his territory he sticks to it year after year. On such a territory a tiger will live alone or with a small group of females. In India, during the dry hot season, lasting from March to June, tigers often congregate beside rivers that have not dried up. There they can bathe and drink and take refuge in the

Although silent and invisible, the moment the tiger sets off to hunt for prey, the animals in the jungle give warning signals. The birds chirp shrilly, and the monkeys rush, shrieking, to the tops of the trees. Some experienced hunters make use of these warning signals to

(Right-hand page)
The tiger probably originated in eastern Siberia. From there it must have gradually emigrated southward and westward. It is built to stand cold better than heat, although it is not to be found above an altitude of 6,500

(Pages 38–39)
In contrast to other cats, the tiger is not afraid of water. It seeks out rivers where it swims with sureness and speed, both on the surface and in the depths.

Through thick vegetation with its patch-work of light and shadow, the tiger can approach close to its victim. It creeps stealthily with an occasional muffled growl, leaps upon its prey, and kills with a blow.

cool shade at the water's edge. The tiger marks his territory with his urine and by standing against the trunks of trees and ripping the bark with his claws.

But he does not climb trees, and one way to keep out of a tiger's way is to climb up a tree. If the tiger does want to get off the ground he finds a sloping trunk. He will mark trees with his claws at a height of six feet from the ground.

Apart from being a poor climber the tiger is in every other way a typical cat. Despite his size, his movements are sinuous, supple and svelte. He can move at great speed. He is an expert stalker, crawling without noise in any kind of cover and flattening himself into invisibility even where cover is scant. He is a first-rate jumper and it has been calculated from tracks that he can leap a distance of as much as fifteen feet.

The hunting tiger stalks to within 20 yards of his prey then closes on it with swift bounds. He will travel up to six miles in a night.

Like the other cats, he is more than a stalker. He will lie up for a prey and attack from ambush. As one would expect, waterholes are much used for this purpose; so are the pathways used by wild game going to such waterholes.

Most animals, with the exception of the elephant and the buffalo, fear the tiger and react with sharp cries of warning at the sound of one. Experienced hunters, when trailing a tiger, rely greatly on the reactions of deer, peacocks and other birds, and especially on the warning cries of monkeys, to guide them to where the big cat is lying up or hiding.

The call of the tiger bears no comparison to the lion's roar. It is a series of harsh growls, sometimes like a fit of coughing.

The tiger's most important senses are smell and hearing. His eyes are not so good; but this is not a great disadvantage to an animal living in dense forest where the field of vision is much reduced. It is more important that he should be able to plot the position of a quarry by nose or ears.

Since time immemorial, the tiger has figured prominently in legend and superstition. In some parts of India, he is looked upon as a god. He is referred to by many names but never by his real one. Asians refer to him as Lord or Master. The Manchus are convinced that the older the tiger, the more

(Above)
When it has spotted its prey, the tiger roars, its hair bristling, its ears cocked, its tail extended. It is about to pounce on its victim and cut its throat with its terrible fangs.

majesty he assumes and that he should certainly be treated with great deference. Sometimes they even go so far as to confer the honorary office of Supreme Governor of the City on a tiger. The inhabitants of the Amur region have so much respect for the tiger that they worship him almost as a god; but most people respect him because they fear him. They are convinced that anyone who kills a tiger will in turn be killed by another tiger. This fear is so great that it even applies to the tiger's footprint, which some people pay homage to. In Sumatra many people believe the tiger to be the reincarnation of a dead person's soul. In India there are innumerable legends about the tiger similar to those in Europe concerning the werewolf.

Over the centuries the tiger has been much hunted—so much so that it is now a rare animal, protected because it is threatened with extinction. Asian monarchs used to arrange tiger hunts, the main features of which were their rowdiness. The Jesuit Verbiest tells us that in the 17th century the Emperor of China mustered a veritable army in the province of Leaotong to hunt tigers. On that one hunt they killed 60 tigers, more than 1,000 deer and a large number of bears and pigs.

The Indian princes used to hunt the tiger with nets. They fixed tall bamboo canes into the ground, about 14 feet apart, and then wound strong nets between them. At each end they erected high platforms where expert riflemen were stationed to wait for the tiger. The tiger was driven by beaters into the net where it was immediately shot.

Only the most self-reliant and single-minded of hunters will go off on his own, on foot, to hunt tigers in an area of thick cover and tall grasses. As a rule, hunters use elephants to track down the tiger; then, at nightfall, they climb into a tree to wait for it. Before doing so they put down the carcass of a freshly killed animal at the foot of the tree as a bait. They may even use a live animal such as a kid or goat. The hunter sits in the tree and waits for the tiger to appear. The bait usually lures the animal within gunshot.

Many types of traps are used to catch tigers, but in the old days the pit trap was the one mainly used. The hunters dug a deep pit in which they placed sharp pointed stakes. The tiger was impaled when he fell through the flimsy grass cover. This method of hunting was prohibited because it resulted in accidents to so many people.

The inhabitants of Java built large cages out of tree trunks and placed live goats inside as a bait. When the tiger entered the cage to attack the bait the cage door closed like a rat-trap and he

(Left)
The tiger is exceptionally strong. It runs ver
swiftly but it does not climb trees. It is said
that it sharpens its claws on the bark of certain
trees, because the crimson sap looks like blood.

(Top)
The choice prey of the tiger are the wild boar,
the deer and antelopes. In times of famine,
however, it eats anything that walks or flies.
It sometimes attacks buffalo, elephants and

(Above)
After it has eaten, the tiger likes to find a
peaceful, secluded spot to rest. It is able to do
without food for quite a long period—a great
advantage in face of the uncertainties of
hunting.

was well and truly imprisoned there.

Local people usually have some idea where tigers are lying up (at least in general terms) and are familiar with many of their habits. For instance they will wander noisily through the forest in single file knowing that the tiger will not attack a party of men who proclaim their presence so noisily. But they also know that only a madman would try to pursue a wounded tiger.

A wounded tiger usually hides in thick cover, such as bushes or dry grass, and will pounce without warning on an inexperienced hunter trying to track him down. However wary of man he may have been, such a tiger will not hesitate to grapple with a hunter when fighting for his life. The man will almost certainly be seriously wounded if not killed in such a grapple.

As a result of hunting, the tiger population of Asia is now estimated at between 10,000 and 20,000. If the species is to be saved from extinction at least as much effort must be put into protecting it as was once put into killing it.

In any confrontation between man and tiger the big cat is as likely to go as to stay to argue. An observer told the story of a tiger that had denned up near a village and was driven from it by small boys throwing stones at it. On another occasion he watched a cattle herder showering insults at a tiger that had just taken one of his heifers. The herder struck the tiger with his stick, forcing it to release the heifer.

Tigers are sometimes arbitrarily divided into three classes: those that prey on

wild game, those that kill cattle, and the smaller number that kill man.

The first group is found in uninhabited areas. They live in the forest and hunt all kinds of wild game. As a result they are looked upon by hunters as competitors. On the other hand they are of great use to farmers because of their predation on wild pigs and other ungulates.

The second category settles near villages and preys mainly upon domestic livestock turned out to pasture. The tiger usually attacks just before dusk. Before nightfall the cattle herders lead their flocks to shelter. Despite this predation on domestic stock, native farmers are mostly against tiger hunting because they look upon the cats as a great asset to agriculture. When the great Don tiger, renowned for such raids, was killed by Sanderson, the natives assembled round the body to apologize for what had happened and to lament the tiger's death. The tiger looms so large in folklore and legend, and is held in such esteem, that this ritual of apologizing to a dead tiger, or

to one about to be killed—even if it is a man-eater—is common in India.

The tiger usually drags his prey into heavy cover where he can eat in peace. A mature tiger at the height of his strength can drag a prey weighing 400 pounds for a distance of 300 yards or more. He takes a long time over his meal, leaving his prey at regular intervals to drink. When drinking, he plunges his head into the water up to the eyes and laps noisily. A mature tiger will consume up to 66 pounds of meat at one meal. During the meal he will even play with the prey or spend much time licking it with his tongue, which is as rough as a grater. Once he has gorged himself, the tiger lies down in some sheltered spot close to the water and spends the next three or four days digesting his meal. A long fast is no upset to him. Tigers in zoos, where they are regularly fed, eat about 14 pounds of raw meat each day. The ability to fast for long periods is a valuable asset to any predator hunting wild game.

Man uses nearly every part of the

tiger's body. In India the fat is especially prized, being considered a most effective remedy for arthritis and cattle diseases. Tiger meat is exported from India to many parts of the world. In Siberia, the meat is reserved for the hunters who have killed the beast, or for old men who were once hunters. Ingenious people consider that tiger flesh provides the human body with the strength and courage needed for hunting it.

In China, the tiger has a therapeutic role. His kneecaps, and the first two ribs, are claimed to have many curative qualities. In other countries use is made of the tiger's claws and liver. The Indian Shikaris keep the canine teeth as precious charms. The women of Asia and Europe wear his claws as ornaments. And of course the skin of the tiger is becoming more and more highly valued by the fur trade throughout the world. Indeed the fur trade, unless halted, could cause the death of this species.

It is always difficult to estimate the life span of a wild animal and this is as true of tigers as of anything else. Sander-

(Top, left)
The largest tigers inhabit the coldest regions of Siberia. Their coat is thick and pale. In the torrid jungle, the tiger is always looking for cool places, and often bathes in the water.

(Left)
The coat hue of tigers varies according to the latitude and climate. Some albino specimens exist, like the one in our photograph, but they are rare. Such animals are especially worshipped by the natives.

(Above)
The tiger needs, in order to survive, a humid climate, very thick vegetation, abundant game and waterholes where it can bathe and quench its thirst.

son reports killing an old animal in Mysore that had been known in the district for 20 years. This animal showed no obvious signs of old age. On the contrary—he appeared to be at the height of his strength and possessed an excellent set of teeth. Only his coat showed signs of losing its bloom.

The mating season in tigers varies from one part of their range to another. In northerly areas, mating takes place in winter; in the south births occur throughout the year. During the mating season, the tiger's cry is heard more frequently than at other times. The court-ship period is two weeks or less. The tigress displays to the tiger, swishing her tail across his back. She rolls on the ground and rubs herself against tree trunks. Attendant tigers fight each other, sometimes fiercely, until only one remains.

After mating the tigress becomes aggressive toward the male and the couple separate. There are occasions on record where she has tried to kill her mate. The adult male, the holder of the territory, will share his range with one or more females but will not accept young males.

The gestation period is 105 to 113 days, which is a short pregnancy for such a large animal. The usual litter is two or three cubs but four, five and six are on record. When the tigress has a very large litter, she may devour some of her young—a pattern perhaps designed to limit the number of mouths in case there should be a food shortage.

The cubs weigh about three pounds at birth which means they are about the size of a small cat. They are born with their eyes closed or half open. The eyes are fully opened within a week, and certainly under a fortnight, but the cubs remain short-sighted for several weeks thereafter. Weaning begins at about six weeks of age, when the cubs are fed partly by meat regurgitated by the tigress; but they suckle her for a long time afterwards. At the age of four months they can accompany their mother on hunting expeditions. Then she teaches them how to dismember prey. Some tigresses will carry animals back to the cubs. At eight months old the cubs are independent.

In contrast to the lion, the tiger usually lives a solitary existence outside the breeding season. It is the tigress who teaches the cubs all they need to know about hunting and killing. It is not uncommon however to see a tiger and a tigress hunting together for several days at a time, or two or three males associating with one female for a short period. Occasionally an old male or female can be seen with grown-up young, but this is unusual, although it does indicate that the tiger can be monogamous at times. In Siberia, where tigers are fewer, monogamy is probably the rule.

Tigers do well in captivity provided they have been caught before the age of two months. They become attached to the person looking after them and follow him about. It is possible to train tigers for circus acts but there is always some risk with this cat because it never really loses its suspicions of man.

In captivity the tiger will live in company with other cats and under such conditions lions and tigers have paired successfully. It has been found easier to cross a lion with a tigress than a tiger with a lioness. Depending on which way the cross has been made the offspring are called tigons or ligers.

46

Tiger cubs are born blind, the size of cats, and clumsy. The mother never leaves their side for the first few weeks, unless hunger forces her out. Her den is usually in the depth of the forest.

(Right)
The gestation is about 100 days. The young are born in inaccessible places. When the cubs are four months old, the female takes them hunting and teaches them to dismember prey.

48 *The tiger often interrupts its meals to go and drink. It plunges its head into the water up to its eyes and laps water noisily. While its food is being digested, it goes to sleep, only waking up to go and drink again.*

Leopards adapt themselves easily to every kind
of habitat. They live in mountains where there
is a shortage of water, in the savanna and in
forests, in hot, humid regions and in deserts.

49

Leopard or Panther

Although there is a tendency nowadays among zoologists to call the leopard a panther the name is not in general use. We speak of the African leopard, the Indian leopard, and the black panther, as though they were three different species when in fact they are really geographical races of one species—the leopard or panther.

Ever since the time of Aristotle there has been confusion about this big cat's name. The ancients believed that the panther was derived from the lion and gave it the name leopard—from *leo* the lion and *pardus* the panther. Nowadays, despite the zoologists, the name leopard is still used by the fur trade.

This is the most widely distributed of all the big cats and can lay claim perhaps to being the most beautiful. If we think of the lion as the king of beasts, and the tiger as the most dangerous or the ocelot as the most beautifully furred, the leopard surely surpasses them all in grace, suppleness and agility. The spotted coat of the leopard makes it highly prized in the fur trade and it looks as though this may cause its extinction.

The so-called black panther is merely a melanistic variety of the leopard and, although black types are more common in Asia than elsewhere, they are liable to turn up in any litter. Melanism, like albinism, is a genetic factor, and the phenomenon of melanism is quite common among cats. Any spotted leopard is liable to produce a litter containing black and spotted cubs.

Leopards are found in the whole of Africa and in Asia Minor, Persia, Transcaucasia up to the Caucasus, in India, the Indian Highlands, China, Manchuria, Siberia and Korea. As a result of this wide distribution, animals in one region vary remarkably from those in another, so it is easy to understand why so many races have been described. After all, the difference in climate between Siberia and tropical Africa is substantial.

The leopards of Siberia and China have much thicker and longer coats than the animals of the tropics. The Saunai leopard, once found in Saunai and in the northern parts of Saudi Arabia, is

The leopard is both slender and robust. It looks like a huge spotted cat, and has the cat's supple, graceful movements.

now an extremely rare animal and may in fact be extinct. Another rare race is the Arabian leopard. Its range extends from the Arabian Peninsula to the Yemen and Oman. It was heavily persecuted by hunting and is extremely rare.

The Anatilian leopard was once found throughout Western Asia Minor and the Transcaucasian republics of the U.S.S.R. It is now extinct in the Caucasus but still survives in small numbers in Turkey, and perhaps in Syria. In Turkey, attempts are being made to save it.

The Amur leopard ranged through Korea, Manchuria and part of the U.S.S.R. east of the Amur River. There are a few of them left now in Korea and north of Vladivostok.

The Barbary leopard, once found in Morocco, Algeria and Tunisia, is found now in only two areas—the Central Atlas mountains and the forests of Oulms.

The most distinctive type is the so-

called black panther, which is not a race but a hue variant. The Indians call it Baghira. The black is caused by an excess of pigment in the coat. The difference between a black panther and the ordinary spotted leopard is no more significant than the difference between a black-haired and a fair-haired human being. The offspring of the black leopard may or may not be black.

A fully grown leopard measures about eight feet in length, including its tail of three feet. The fur is yellow or dark yellow and the long body, including the head, is spotted with black. On the back and along the flanks, the spots form rings and the fur inside the rings is darker than that outside. The jaguar, another big cat, is similarly marked but has dark dots inside the black rings. The weight of an adult leopard varies from 130 to 180 pounds. Melanistic leopards (black panthers) are particularly common in the islands of the Sea of Java and above all in Java itself.

At first sight the leopard's coat may seem too conspicuous for a predator that has to wait long and patiently in a tree for prey to appear. But every hunter knows that the shade of the leopard's coat can appear exactly like the dense dark foliage that screens it.

Its widespread distribution goes hand in hand with an unspecialized ecology.

(Above)
The black panther is especially common on the island of Java and, because of this, used to be known as the panther of the Sunda Islands. Strangely enough it is not found in Sumatra or Borneo.

(Top)
The snow leopard (Panthera uncia) has longer and thicker fur than that of the common leopard. It lives in the mountainous regions of central Asia.

For a long time, the black panther was
thought to be a separate species. Today it is
established that spotted panthers can give
birth to black-coated cubs, due to the
phenomenon of melanism.

So the leopard is at home in the humid forests of Africa and Asia, and in savanna and steppe regions. In agricultural areas leopards often inhabit fields, plantations and groves of low trees. They will live quite happily in mountains where the grassy slopes provide excellent hiding places and abundant and varied prey. In Abyssinia, leopards are found at a height of between 6,000 and 9,000 feet. Many live near human dwellings, and seem to have no fear of man.

One of the leopard's most outstanding characteristics is its amazing mobility. It has exceptional vitality, energy and stamina. It can move fast on the ground and with absolute certainty in the tree-tops. In the latter respect it resembles the smaller cats. It excels at taking game by surprise, even the quickest and most cautious species. It is an excellent climber and will often take refuge in trees when pursued. It is also an excellent swimmer and will cross wide rivers. All its movements are light and precise. It is impressive to watch when running at speed, threading its way skilfully through trees and bushes. The only other carnivore that can match the leopard for this is the genet.

The leopard's style of hunting is to wait in a tree, or belly-crawl towards its prey and strike by means of a long jump. It then carries its prey into the tree—a habit particularly noticeable in African leopards. By this method the leopard protects its prey from hyenas and

(Top)
The leopard, like the cat, has a rounded head with a short snout. Its fangs are relatively more powerful than those of the lion.

(Above)
The speed and precision of the leopard's reflexes are superior to those of other mammals. At the first sign of danger, it disappears in a flash into the thickets.

jackals who would otherwise claim their share. Oddly enough a leopard's prey in a tree is never touched by vultures. Before hoisting its prey on to a high branch to be eaten at leisure, the leopard takes out and buries the entrails.

The leopard has a wide prey range and hunts animals from the smallest to the largest. It kills its victim by breaking its neck; then it cuts its throat and licks the blood. It hunts antelopes, frogs, lizards and mice. It also hunts monkeys and will climb after them into the trees. When a monkey sees a leopard it begins to call in alarm and climbs to the topmost branches. African leopards prey very largely on the sacred baboon. An adult leopard requires from 11 to 13 pounds of meat daily.

If a leopard attacks sheep in a flock it

can cause a real massacre. It will kill a dozen sheep in a night. Shepherds hate it more than any other animal because it does not satisfy itself with one victim.

Like any other beast of prey, or for that matter any other wild animal, the leopard usually tries to avoid man. But, when wounded or brought to bay, it will defend itself, hurling itself furiously at the man who has wounded it. A leopard with young will attack man if they are threatened.

An animal may appear to be making an unprovoked attack simply because its motives are not known. It is a fact, however, that the leopard is bold enough to hunt right into towns and villages and will even go inside houses near large forested areas. It will attack domestic livestock even under the eyes of the

owner. In many parts of Africa the owners shut their domestic animals up at night in special sheds designed to protect them from leopard attacks.

In certain parts of India there used to be much talk about man-eating leopards, and about 1860 there were particularly serious casualties. It is said that one leopard slaughtered 100 sheep in a night before being killed by a Sikh. Another crept through houses at night and attacked the sleeping people. It also attacked guards posted in the fields. For three years this leopard hunted over a territory of about 20 miles, killing more than 200 men.

One of the legends has it that a man and his wife, returning home, suddenly found themselves face to face with a leopard. This filled them with terror.

54

The leopard is the most versatile of the cats. It runs swiftly, leaps easily, climbs trees with agility and swims without difficulty across rivers. It is extremely cunning and hunts all kinds of game.

The man consoled his wife by telling her that he had in his possession a magic powder that would transform him into a panther. He took a pinch of it, giving the rest of it to his wife, who agreed to keep it safely for him. As soon as he had changed into a panther the man succeeded in routing the big cat. But when he turned to his wife for another pinch of the magic powder that would change him back into a man, she was so scared to see him in panther form that she became frightened and threw the powder away. Condemned now to live forever in the form of a panther, the man turned on his wife and killed her, thus starting his career as the terrible man-eating panther of the legend.

The mating season of the leopard is during February and March when several males will pursue a single female, sending up shrill but powerful roars. There is often fierce fighting among these males.

Pairs stay together only for the period of mating. The gestation period is about 15 weeks. Litters vary in size from three to five young, and their eyes open after about ten days.

Leopard cubs are beautiful, with lightly marked silky fur. They play together like kittens and draw their mother into their games. The leopardess lavishes great care and attention upon them and will defend them courageously in circumstances where the tiger might abandon her young.

In the wild she will hide her young in a hole in the rocks, in thick jungle or undergrowth, or in a crude nest built in a tree. As soon as they reach the size of a fully grown domestic cat the mother takes them on hunting trips. During the period when she is suckling her young she can become very ferocious, not hesitating to attack and kill any animal that comes near them.

Because of its great strength, the leopard can kill animals bigger than itself and has been known to carry a carcass weighing well over one hundredweight to a height of 20 feet in a tree. Usually the leopard hunts alone but occasionally groups are reported. They hunt in the early morning and at night, but where they are under pressure from man they become almost entirely nocturnal.

The leopard is not notably territorial, certainly not as territorial as the tiger. It can go for longer periods without

When the leopard is hunting, it watches for the slightest movement of its prey. As soon as an animal comes within reach, it pounces on it and slits its throat. It kills more victims than it can eat and abandons dead animals on the ground.

drinking, and therefore without showing itself, so it is less often seen than most animals. More agile than the tiger, the leopard does not hesitate to attack elephants, and appears always to pick out the leader.

Leopard hunting is considered to be more exciting and more dangerous than tiger hunting, and wherever it lives this big cat is vindictively harassed. In India the Sikhs lay traps for it exactly similar in design to rat-traps. The cat is lured into the traps by a bait of a dog or a kid. In Asia, as in Africa, dogs are widely used in leopard hunting. A leopard surrounded by a pack of barking dogs will take refuge in a tree. It is then easily killed by a rifle or poisoned arrows.

When the great rulers of Asia arranged fights using wild animals they often replaced tigers with leopards. Here is an account of one of these fights that took place in Java:

"Several thousand natives assembled round a well-defined square of grassland which served as a battlefield. These armed Javanese forming the lines were not soldiers, nor hunters paid for their services, but merely young people who fought for the pleasure of the sport. There were about 2,000 of them, armed with lances and particularly numerous round the platforms reserved for the people of importance from the village. Behind them crowded the villagers, climbing up the surrounding trees. In

(Top)
The leopard likes to climb trees, from the top of which it surveys its hunting territory. There it can hide, scarcely visible, among the foliage

(Above)
The leopard moves with great agility on branches of trees. This stands it in good stead when it is fleeing from danger, or when it is lying in wait for its prey.

(Right)
The jaguar's coat is smooth, glossy and tawny with black spots.

the middle of the open space was a large wooden crate in which the leopard was held. Eight natives armed with lances crouched beside it. These were the real warriors. One wore a scarlet jacket and carried a dagger—the famous Malay dagger with a curved blade. After a short ceremony he opened the crate and out came a magnificent leopard. Blinded by the sun, the beast tried at first to go back, but the youth roused it by throwing a stone at it. The animal leapt to one side but it was surrounded by the armed men. The eight fighters advanced slowly towards it and the leopard pounced on them. Hit by two lances, it toppled over backwards, got up again and tried to escape. It hurled itself at the wall of armed men, who drove it away, wounding it again and again. The struggle went on for several hours. At last, marked all over with lance wounds the leopard collapsed."

Hated by the natives because of its predation on their domestic stock, but above all for the terror it rouses in them, the leopard has always been hunted in one way or another. The beauty of its coat has of course intensified this. The highly original patterns on its fur have made it greatly desired since the remotest times—by natives who thought it ideal for covering their warriors' shields.

But hunting for this purpose was limited. Today the whim of fashion has transformed limited hunting into an all-out war and the systematic destruction of leopards for the fur trade has led, in certain regions, to a scarcity that has resulted in great ecological imbalance. This imbalance has serious effects on the vegetation. In the Atlas mountains, for example, the high breeding rate of Barbary apes, and a high survival rate among their young, have put the forests in severe danger. The apes are pulling at the branches and destroying the young shoots. This is the result of the absence of predation by leopards.

Like the lion, the leopard is a common animal in the zoos, where it arrives usually when it is very young or very old. If well looked after it can live for a long time in captivity. This applies to all the races except the snow leopard, which is a distinct species.

The snow leopard, accustomed to living at altitudes of over 6,000 feet, rarely survives for more than one and a

(Pages 58– 9)
When the leopard kills an animal too large to be eaten at a single meal, it hides the remains in the fork of a tree, so that it can return later and finish it off at its leisure.

(Left)
The thick, woolly coat of the snow leopard enables it to stand up to the bitter climate of the mountains of Asia where it lives. Its coat is gray, marked with black rosettes, and with a

The young leopards are born in well-hidden lairs. They feed off their mothers for a long time, and she fusses over them most attentively. When they are about a year old, they learn to hunt and become independent.

half to two years in captivity. This is the more regrettable because, of all the leopards, it is the easiest to tame. Contrary to what one might think it is not temperature that upsets it; it is atmospheric pressure and the percentage of oxygen in the air. At higher altitudes it can live for up to eight years in captivity.

Like all big cats, the leopard needs a warm, clean cage and the right amount of meat. When closely confined, it cries plaintively like a cat. When free, its cry is much harsher. When it is happy it will leap with a boldness and grace that visitors to a zoo love to watch. It chooses the darkest corner of its cage to sleep in. When tired it will climb to the highest point in its cage. This siesta can last all afternoon if the beast is not disturbed. But the leopard's sleep, seemingly so deep, does not prevent it from noticing the minutest noise. Any animal passing near its cage is enough to rouse it.

If captured very young the leopard is easily tamed and there have always been people who have kept them as pets. The pet leopard purrs like a cat. But it is still potentially dangerous and, when adult, can become unpredictable. In Rome quite recently a three year old tame leopard killed a 41 year old maid who was sweeping up. There was no apparent reason for the killing.

Adult leopards are impossible to tame. One man who had lived for a long time in Africa told how he had kept one for years without being able to make friends with it. Whenever he went near its cage it would show its displeasure by grinding its teeth and roaring in a special way. If he pretended to be completely disinterested, the leopard would watch until he was passing its door then it would strike out powerfully at him with its paw. The man had the animal on a long chain so that he could let it out from time to time to exercise in the yard, but it began to leap about like a mad thing, roaring and grinding its teeth in a threatening way, obviously ready to attack anyone. It became extremely difficult to get it back into its cage. Even a whip was useless, but where the whip failed a bucket of water succeeded. When the water was thrown over its head the leopard went back to its cage. Adult leopards are best left to their wild state.

(Left)
The leopard leads a solitary life, although it does hunt in groups at times. It crouches in the branches of trees close to the paths frequented by herbivores, when they are on their way to

(Above)
The fur of the leopard is much sought after. The relatively dark yellow base is covered with ring-shaped black markings enclosing a darker yellow zone. No two furs are identical.

Jaguar

The jaguar (*Panthera onca*) is the most widely distributed of all the New World cats. It is confined to the Americas.

Although it is about the same overall length as the Old World leopard—more than eight feet long plus tail of two and a half feet—it is a much heavier animal, thicker in the body and more powerfully muscled. Weight ranges, according to age and sex, up to 250 pounds. Weights of 250 pounds or over are common enough along the Amazon and in Paraguay. But animals up to 300 pounds have been recorded in Peru. Mexican jaguars are smaller and much lighter in weight.

Despite its weight and its robust build, despite its heavy tread and seeming clumsiness, it can be as agile as the leopard when it has to be or wants to be. Its strength equals that of the lion or the tiger. It has excellent hearing and its sight is above average. As in all the cats, its sense of smell is less good, but it can scent prey at a considerable distance.

The jaguar's fur is short, thick, soft and glossy, longer on the throat and at the base of the neck than on the chest and stomach. There is much variation in coat, which is not surprising considering its wide distribution; but the basic coat is nearly always orange-yellow. The stomach, tip of the muzzle and the inside of the ears are white. The coat is leopard-spotted—some of the spots being small and irregular, while others are large and round, edged with reddish-yellow and enclosing one or more dark points. The markings on the back are set closely together, forming an irregular band that divides on the rump.

Black jaguars are quite common,

commoner than in any other cat. The tendency is for the animals to be darker or blacker in heavy forest. On the other hand, black specimens occur on high, dry, non-forested areas such as north-eastern Brazil. Black jaguars are like black leopards—melanistic variants and not races. This melanism, as in leopards, is due to excess pigment.

In the 17th century, jaguars were extremely common, and it is on record that about 2,000 were killed each year in Paraguay alone. Today they are rarer, and have almost disappeared from many areas. They have become extremely rare in the south-west United States but are more widespread in Mexico. In South America they are found as far as northern Argentina and Paraguay.

This is a cat of the wooded river banks. It likes the forest edge near bogs and marshes where grass and rushes grow six feet tall or higher. It is rarely seen on open plains which it crosses, as a rule, only to get from one place to another.

Hunting time for the jaguar is just before dawn or after dusk, but some-times it will hunt all night. If it is sur-prised by the sunrise away from home, it will stretch out in tall grass or in the heart of some thicket, and spend the daylight hours sleeping there.

Any animal that it can catch and hold is liable to become the jaguar's prey. A common prey species is the capybara—a gigantic guinea-pig-like rodent that lives near rivers and weighs up to and over 100 pounds. The cat stalks silently and takes its victims by surprise. Having broken the neck of the prey, the jaguar then drags it off into the bushes.

Besides stalking prey in this manner, the jaguar can play the same waiting role as other cats, lying in the under-growth, watching patiently, generally waving its tail, waiting for the prey to come to it. Quite often it will lie in ambush at a waterhole where other animals come to drink.

Along river banks it hunts a variety of mammals and marsh birds. It is one of the fishing cats and can scoop fish out of the water with a flick of its paw. Jaguars are known to tap the surface of the water with their tails to attract fish. The tail tapping apparently makes a sound resembling the falling of pods and berries, and attracts species of fish that eat these. There is an Indian tradition

Although they have different coats, these two jaguars could well have been born in the same litter. A large-sized cayman does not frighten them: they tear it to pieces with their claws.

that this cat will also drool spittle onto the water to attract fish.

Although the jaguar takes most of its prey on the ground or in the water, it is, despite its weight, an accomplished climber. If pursued it will seek refuge in a tree. It will also hunt in trees where it catches monkeys and other tree-loving species. Because of its weight, however, it cannot climb onto the higher and more slender branches, so monkeys that can reach the treetops are safe. For the same reason the jaguar is seldom able to catch a sloth. On the ground it takes the biggest prey, including tapirs. Its range is determined more by the presence of suitable prey species than by conditions like climate, forest, swamp, plains or desert.

Small prey is eaten entirely, including skin and bones, but the jaguar does not eat every animal it kills. Once it has finished a meal it retires into the forest, where it sleeps not far from its prey. That evening or the following morning it returns to the carcass, eats a little more and leaves the rest for the vultures. It is usually content to avoid man or, at the most, to watch him from a distance. Where much persecuted, it becomes entirely nocturnal. When wounded it will rarely attack man, and eats him only in the most exceptional circumstances.

The jaguar's roar cannot, in any way, compare with the roar of the lion. In fact, like the leopard and the tiger, it is a relatively quiet animal. At most, it utters a low-key growl and rarely raises the pitch of this cry. It can, however, be located by the noise that monkeys make when they spot it below, on the prowl.

Where food is sufficiently abundant, and where it is not disturbed by man, the jaguar tends to be territorial and remains in one place. It moves only if game becomes rare—and always at night.

It is a very good swimmer and is able to cross the widest rivers. It is at its most dangerous when it is in the water. If it thinks it is being pursued, or has been wounded, it will attack a boat. The wounds it inflicts on the people in the boat are always potentially dangerous because of their effects. If not treated at once, they can lead to tetanus.

Outside the breeding season the jaguar is usually a solitary animal although there have been reports from time to time of small units resembling a pride of lions.

66

The jaguar is the largest of the New World cats. It lives in South and Central America, where it has long been hunted.

cubs become like the adult jaguars.

Jaguar cubs can be easily tamed if taken very young. They play quite happily with puppies and kittens. Their movements are quick and graceful. They quickly learn to recognize their owner, seeking him out and showing great pleasure in his company. They breed well in captivity and can be crossed with leopards.

Because of the damage they do among flocks of sheep and cattle, jaguars have always been hunted by man. South American Indians hunt them with arrows poisoned with curare. Sometimes they are hunted with hounds, but this can be extremely dangerous. Once the jaguar has been brought to bay the hunters stab it with a special, double-bladed dagger, protecting their arms with sheepskin while doing so. The dogs then kill the wounded animal.

The gauchos of Paraguay hunt the jaguar on horseback. They lasso it, then drag it along the ground until it is dead.

The fur trade is, today, the jaguar's most serious enemy. Its beautiful fur is much sought after, and the demand for pelts has led to a serious decline in its numbers. In South America, the skin is used for rugs.

In the mating season, it tends to be more gregarious. Then groups of eight, nine or ten animals may be seen together, but not for long.

In tropical areas jaguars seem to breed at any time of the year. On the perimeter of their range they breed in spring. The gestation period is about 14 weeks. The usual litter is two cubs, sometimes three, which are born in the thickest undergrowth of the forest or in hollows near half-uprooted trees.

The mother stays with her family for the first few days of their lives. If they are threatened, or she thinks they are threatened, she will carry them off by the scruff of the neck. She defends them boldly and will drive off any enemy or intruder. By the time they are six months old the young follow their mother on hunting trips. At first they keep to the cover of the thickets, then they take part in ambushes. They are deserted by their mother as soon as they are able to hunt. Up to the age of seven months they have a long woolly coat, heavily spotted. After that age the

When one watches a young jaguar playing in the grass like a large, rather clumsy cat, it is hard to imagine that, when fully grown, it will be celebrated for its strength.

Genus felis

The cats of this genus are small to medium size, similar in structure and general habits. There is little fundamental difference for example between the ordinary domestic cat and the handsome puma, and their hunting methods are similar.

We shall now describe the puma, the jaguarondi, the ocelot, the fisher cat, the serval, the wildcat, gloved cat, the lynx, caracal and the domestic cats.

Puma

The puma (*Felis concolor*) is a New World cat with many names—cougar, mountain-lion, silver lion, panther and painter, the last name being a corruption of the term panther. It is almost as widely distributed as the jaguar, and was once found from Alaska to Tierro del Fuego, in the forests of Canada, in the jungles of the Amazon, on the South American pampas and the high plateaux of the Andes. Hunting and the extension of cultivated areas have exterminated it over much of North America. But it is still widespread in British Columbia, Central and South America as far south as the Argentine.

This handsome cat has been subjected to the scientific ritual of sub-specification. At least 15 races have been described and twice as many sub-species have actually been given names. There are certainly several geographical races differing in size and hue. Of these, the biggest is the Canadian puma which is silver-gray. South American pumas are smaller and rusty-brown.

The Florida cougar (puma) is a sub-species that was once thought to be extinct, but it is now known to exist in the Everglades and may well be able to build up its numbers in the Everglades National Park. This sub-species used to be found as far west as the Western Mississippi. The Florida cougar measures up to seven feet in overall length. It is the brightest of all the sub-species.

The Eastern cougar, whose range once extended from south-eastern United States to Canada and the Western plains, was reckoned to be extinct by 1900. However it is still found in Canada and seems to be holding on in some parts of the United States.

As a general rule, pumas are bigger in the colder parts of their range and smaller in the tropics. A mature puma of the larger races will measure up to five feet in length plus three feet of tail. The smallest races may be as small as four feet in overall length, that is including tail. The weight range is equally wide, the smallest specimens weighing under 50 pounds, while the biggest ever recorded specimen weighed 260 pounds.

The puma has a distinctive profile, very like the profile of a Siamese cat. In fact, the Siamese cat is sometimes described as puma-faced. Most commonly it is a handsome tawny-red, dark on the back and becoming brownish-white on the stomach. The fur is paler on the chest and becomes white on the throat, around the mouth and inside the ears. There is a small white patch above and below the eyes. In general, the coat of

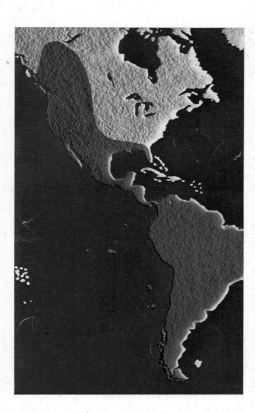

(Left)
In the forests, the jaguar hides itself in the tall grass, close to the marshes. It goes out hunting at night, killing anything that comes its way—mammals, fish, birds, tortoises or

(Top)
The distribution area of the puma extends from Canada to Patagonia and includes both mountains and plains, humid forests and desert steppes, tropical zones and the regions of

(Above)
Despite its suspicious attitude, this young puma is only too happy to be tamed, and even adult pumas do not attack man.

The puma looks like a small lioness with its tawny coat and its similarly shaped body. This is why it is called the mountain lion.

the puma is not unlike that of the lion after which it is sometimes named. There is no difference between the coats of the male and the female.

The puma breeds in any month of the year. The gestation period is 13 weeks. Litter size varies from one or two up to three and, occasionally, four cubs. The cubs are born with their eyes closed and have a spotted coat and a black, ringed tail. The spots and the black rings disappear as they mature. At birth, they are the size of a six weeks old domestic kitten. They are big-footed and clumsy, and stagger awkwardly, constantly falling over each other when following their mother. At the age of five or six weeks, they play about the den mouth. Between the 10th and the 12th weeks, they take on their adult coats.

It is often said that female pumas kill the young of their first litter, but this is by no means certain. A number of cats, including the tiger, are known to kill kittens for one reason or another. It would be surprising if pumas were any different, killing first litters as a ritual. The female puma, in fact, is a most attentive mother and cares for her young until they are two years old. Young pumas are known to hunt together for a short time.

Outside the breeding season, pumas lead solitary lives, males and females meeting only for the purpose of mating. They rarely settle for long between breeding seasons and there is no indication of territorial activity.

The puma is a quick, powerful cat, as much at home in the trees as it is on the ground. During the day, it sleeps in trees and it will attack prey from there. It will also be found lying up by day in dense undergrowth or tall grass. It hunts usually at night. It can leap 12 feet into the air and cover 20 feet at a bound. The biggest pumas are reputed to be able to make even greater bounds than this.

Where deer are numerous they make up much of the puma's diet. It also feeds on agoutis, sheep, rabbits and monkeys. The agility of the monkeys is little use to them because the puma is as much at home in the trees as they. It can leap from tree to tree with the greatest of ease, even where the branches are thick and entangled.

Although it can create havoc among herds of cattle and will even kill foals,

the puma usually confines its attacks to animals from the size of a sheep down. When it has captured a prey, it cuts its throat and drinks the blood.

Mainly a night hunter, the puma sees better in the twilight and in the dark than it does by day. Its sense of smell is not acute but its hearing is remarkably so. It is an excellent swimmer but apparently swims only when it is absolutely necessary.

This cat has always been notable for its generally neutral attitude to man. If captured when very young, pumas are easily tamed. They live amicably with dogs and domestic cats but, like foxes, they cannot resist killing domestic poultry. Like domestic cats, they can amuse themselves for hours, playing with balls

of wool and other objects. Despite their size, they can safely be given the freedom of the house. They will seek out their master because they enjoy his company. They purr when petted and some hunters claim that they are noisy animals in the wild state.

Jaguarondi

The Jaguarondi (*Felis jaguarondi*) is an extremely agile, fleet-footed American cat with a long, weasel-like body, a long tail and short legs. It has a small, wide, flattened head, small low-set ears and round eyes. It is more weasel-like than cat-like, and closely resembles the marten.

The fur is short, thick and dark

(Top)
The puma sleeps during the day in the trees, in bushes or hidden in tall grasses. Like so many of the cats, it is a nocturnal animal.

(Above)
Although the jaguarondi is undoubtedly a cat, it looks more like a marten with its short legs and long tail.

brownish-gray, sometimes indistinctly blotched or striped. It looks darker when the fur is groomed and the dark tips can be seen, much lighter when the hair is raised to reveal the pale roots. Females are generally paler than males.

This cat is smaller than the smallest puma, varying in length from 18 inches to two feet. The tail is 15 inches or a little longer. Height at the shoulder is about 15 inches.

Jaguarondi are found in Mexico and a large part of South America, ranging in fact, from the southern United States through Central America as far as Paraguay and Central and Northern Argentina.

The habitat of the jaguarondi is the forest fringe. It is also found in savanna grasslands, but is not fond of wide open spaces with sparse cover.

It hunts at dawn and twilight but is reluctant to come out in bad weather and will not emerge until hunting conditions are right. It is a good climber and moves at considerable speed on the ground despite its short legs. It preys mainly on birds and smaller mammals like rats, agoutis and rabbits. It is said to be able to kill prey up to the size of a calf.

This is a territorial species, but not aggressively so. The animals live in pairs and they are as permanently settled as badgers. Unlike other wild cats, jaguarondi couples often share their hunting range with other couples.

When her young are due, the female jaguarondi prepares her nursery in the heart of the forest, in a ditch lined with branches or in a hollow tree. The gestation period is nine or ten weeks, and the normal litter is two or three.

Jaguarondi never attack human beings and they are not dangerous when being hunted or when wounded. They are trapped and hunted with hounds. As a rule, the jaguarondi will try to escape by hiding in the undergrowth when hard pressed. But it is just as likely to climb into a tree or leap into the water and save itself by swimming.

If captured young, jaguarondi are easily tamed and soon become as friendly as domestic cats. But it is unwise to give them complete freedom of movement because sometimes they can be savage. They cannot be broken of the habit of chasing poultry or ducks.

When eating, the jaguarondi holds its

The jaguarondi is twice as large as a domestic cat. Seen here on the ground, it is essentially an arboreal animal.

food in its forepaws and chews it like the domestic cat. Once it has eaten its fill it licks its paws carefully and goes to sleep. In cold weather, it will curl up into a ball with its tail clasped like a dormouse. In warm weather it stretches out, with paws outstretched and tail extended.

Ocelot *(Felis pardalis)*

The ocelot, called *tlalocelotl* by the Mexicans, is a big American cat with a handsome coat. Because of its handsome coat, it is much sought after by the fur trade. Because it tames readily if taken

young, it is much in demand as a household pet.

As a counter to this trend, attempts are being made to breed the ocelot in zoos. One pair has bred regularly in captivity in Scotland but, so far as is known, this has been the only success in the United Kingdom.

This is a long-legged cat, built like a lynx, with a powerful body and heavy, thick-set head. Fully grown, it can measure over five feet in overall length. The tail is about 15 inches long. Height at the shoulder is about 18 inches. Fully grown, the ocelot can weigh 35 pounds.

The handsome coat, which is short-haired, thick and silky, shows great variation—from light gray or yellowish-gray to a rich brown. The fur is golden on the head and the middle of the back, and silvery on the sides. On the body it is marked with rows of irregular brown blotches, ringed with black. On the head and chest, these become black pencillings. There are white marks on the back of the ears. The body markings are more pronounced in males than in females. In females, the shoulders and the rump are dappled with round spots. But the pattern of the ocelot's fur varies so much

The ocelot is one of the largest felines in America. Its magnificent coat is in such demand that today the species is threatened with extinction.

73

that it is impossible to find two identical animals.

Although it is becoming increasingly rare, the ocelot is still widely distributed, ranging from Mexico and the southwest United States, through Central America, south to Paraguay and northern Argentina. It is not found in the West Indies.

The ocelot is never found in treeless areas, so it is absent from the plains. It is a forest cat, found almost always near human habitations. Where it is not persecuted, it hunts by day, but, when under pressure, as when it is being hunted for its fur, it becomes nocturnal. It now has the reputation of hunting only on the darkest nights. During the day it lies up in thick undergrowth or in trees. It does not appear to be territorial.

Males and females usually hunt separately, but sometimes in pairs. Although they can catch birds and small mammals in the trees, they do most of their hunting on the ground. They have a wide prey range. Apart from birds killed in the nest, in trees or on the forest floor, they take agoutis, monkeys, rodents, brocket deer and reptiles. They prey upon domestic stock, including poultry.

Male and female ocelot will help each other against a common enemy. The ocelot is not dangerous to man and runs away at once from his dogs. It is easily trapped and is often caught in pairs when raiding poultry houses.

This cat is said to breed twice a year. Two kittens are normal. The female ocelot hides her kittens in the forest depths or in the hollow of a tree. As soon as they are weaned, she carries small birds and mammals to them.

Because of its handsome appearance, the ocelot is much in demand as a household pet. Unfortunately, when taken young, it adapts quickly to a domestic life and becomes as playful as a young cat. So the demand goes on and the population dwindles. Older ocelots are less easily tamed. No ocelot ever grows out of the habit of chasing domestic livestock. As they grow older, domesticated ocelots become unpredictable and sometimes dangerous.

Fisher Cat (Felis viverrina)

Of all the Asiatic wild cats, the fisher cat is the one that most closely resembles the domestic cat in size and structure. It is about two and a half feet long with a tail of 12 inches and its weight is about 16 pounds. In general appearance, it is not unlike the leopard.

Judged by its coat, this is probably the least attractive of all the cats. The fur is rough, lifeless and short, grayish-brown or grayish-yellow, with black spots that sometimes become stripes. The whole body is covered by these dark stipples which sometimes form close series. The stippling continues along the back. There are horizontal stripes on the paws. The tail has eight or nine dark rings. The pupils of the eyes are round, not almond-shaped, and the iris is bronze.

The fisher cat is found in India, Ceylon, Nepal, Indo-China, Sumatra and Java. Its habitat is rain-forest, especially near river mouths. It is especially fond of marshy places because, unlike other cats, it feeds to a considerable extent on fish, which it catches with great skill. But it

(Above)
In spite of its small size, the fisher cat is very aggressive. It has strong teeth and preys upon fish, birds and mammals.

(Top, left)
Just as playful as a cat, and miaowing and purring like one, the ocelot adapts itself easily to captivity. Since it is a nocturnal animal, however, it sleeps throughout the day.

also feeds on big snails, small mammals and birds. Despite its small size, it is very aggressive and does not hesitate to attack animals bigger than itself. It is even said to face man. In captivity, it remains savage and does not readily tolerate the presence of human beings.

Serval (Felis serval)

The serval is bigger than the European wildcat, but smaller than the lynx. It stands about 20 inches tall at the shoulder and its overall length is about 4 feet, including its tail of 12 inches. It is a slim, long-legged cat with large, oval, up-pointing ears. In many ways it resembles the South American ocelot.

The fur of the serval is reddish or yellowish on the back and white on the underside—short, dense and glossy. Along its back, there are black spots in regular rows. The spotting becomes irregular on the flanks, the neck and the legs. The serval's tail is black-ringed.

This is an African cat, found in South-West and East Africa and as far north as Algeria.

The Barbary serval, a longer-coated cat, is now extremely rare and found only in the humid forest area of Algeria.

The habitat of the serval is bushed savanna, the forest fringe and high moorlands. It likes to be within easy reach of water, so is particularly fond of marshy places with long grass or reeds. In mountain areas, it ranges up to the 6,000 feet contour where it dens in rock clefts or caves.

During the day, the serval lies up in deep shade, emerging about twilight to hunt. It has a wide prey range, from small antelopes down to small mammals and lizards. Having a considerable turn of speed, it is able to course hares as the cheetah does. It kills rats, guineafowl and other birds. When hunting birds, it is able to catch them on the wing,

(Top)
If the serval is captured when young, it can be very easily tamed. Here we see the small size of its head and the length of its neck and legs.

(Above)
When it is still very young, the serval cub is already able to climb trees. Later on, when adult, it will drop from the branches onto its victim without warning. Ambushing in this way is its preferred form of hunting.

leaping up to a height of six feet to do so. But, like other cats, it will lie in ambush and wait for the prey to come to it.

A serval lying in ambush is difficult to see, so it is not an easy animal to watch when it is hunting. Africans hunt it with dogs and the hunted serval will seek refuge in a tree. It is also widely trapped for its fur, which is known in the fur trade as cape cat. As a result of continued hunting pressure, the serval has now become extremely rare except in Somaliland and Eritrea. In East Africa, its flesh is eaten, except by Muslims.

The female gives birth to her young in a rock crevice or a grassy hollow or in the deserted burrow of a porcupine or ant-bear. The gestation period is two and a half months, and there are two to four kittens in a litter.

If captured young and well cared for, the serval tames easily. But it does not tame if taken as an adult.

European Wildcat

A fully grown wildcat can reach the size of an average fox. By any yardstick, it is bigger and more powerfully built than any domestic cat—big-skulled, wide-eared, moon-eyed and with ringed, club tail. It has bigger whiskers, thicker fur and more powerful teeth. Its black ringed tail is as thick at the tip as at the base, while that of the domestic cat is long and tapering.

Nevertheless, for a very long time, it was believed that the European wildcat (*Felis sylvestris*) was the ancestor of the domestic cat. This idea, despite all the superficial resemblances, has now been abandoned. But it is a fact that the wildcat and the domestic cat can interbreed —and sometimes do so in the Scottish Highlands. The Scottish race of the wildcat is known as *Felis sylvestris grampia*.

There is some variation in hue and in markings, and considerable variation in weight, between one part of the cat's range and another. Common weights are 10 to 12 pounds but some cats reach 15 pounds. Overall length is three feet to four feet, including 12 to 14 inches of tail. In Europe, exceptional specimens have reached nearly five feet in overall length. The animal's height at the

76 *The wildcat, which is a forest dweller, takes cover in the trees, and will lie there patiently waiting for its prey.*

(Pages 78–9)
The mother puma is capable of providing for an additional animal as well as for her own family as, for example, this lynx, so long as it does not threaten her own offspring.

When the young pumas are born, they have dark spots on their coats. They are blind and can do nothing but lurch around. After three months, they shed their first fur and their coat becomes plain like their parents'. They have excellent eyesight and are agile enough to follow their mother on hunting expeditions.

The caracal is impatient to eat a hare it has just caught. It seems quite unafraid of the watching photographer. With its powerful leg muscles, the caracal can avoid danger by leaping from sight with a single leap.

shoulder varies from 14 to 16 inches.

The fur of the wildcat is grayish-tawny, very often grayish-yellow in females, and marked with crosswise dark stripes. The throat has yellowish-white spots. The skin on the nose is pink. There is a dark line along the back as far as the base of the tail. The flanks are tiger-striped; the leg striping is horizontal. The soles of the feet are dark brown. The ears, which are parted and lie back, are grayish-rust on the outside and gray on the inside.

The wildcat is rarer in Europe than it used to be, but is still widely distributed. It is not found in Arctic regions; but occurs in the Ukraine, the Caucasus and Asia Minor. It is common in the Scottish Highlands. Although wildcats prefer mountain forests, they show great adaptability and have long survived in the Scottish Highlands on high, treeless ground. The den is among rocks or in a hole in a tree, but the cat will occupy the burrows of other animals, especially in cold weather.

Wildcats are solitary animals, and it is uncommon to see two together except in the brief period of mating. When the female has her kittens, she is settled until they are off her hands. The males are great wanderers and sometimes cover considerable distances.

In Europe, the mating season is in February, and the kittens are born in April. The gestation period is nine weeks. In Scotland, there appears to be no fixed mating season, as kittens are found in many months of the year. In this respect, the wildcat may be like the otter. Some observers consider that Scottish wildcats can have two litters in a year. The wildcat will sometimes interbreed with the domestic cat and hybrids are not uncommon.

The female cat chooses for her nursery a rock cleft or a hollow tree. Litter size varies from three to five or six young, which are born with their eyes closed. Once they are weaned the mother brings them rats, voles, rabbits and small birds. The kittens very quickly begin to climb trees. The branches soon become their main playground and their best hiding place. The wildcat is expert at concealing itself among foliage.

Most people see a wildcat when it is being hunted or has been brought to bay on a rock face or in a tree by terriers.

(Top)
The tail of the wildcat is very bushy and as thick at the tip as at the base, in contrast to that of gone-wild domestic cats, which is tapered.

(Above)
The wildcat has an orange snout and pink nose. The ears lie well back, sometimes almost horizontal, and its throat has whitish markings on it.

81

Then it is a snarling spitfire, and most photographs of wildcats show it in this pose. But it is no more a habitual snarler than the domestic cat. It will face dogs when brought to bay but, if there is an escape route, it will take it rather than fight. The female cat, despite her attachment to her kittens, will abandon them if she is too hard pressed.

It has always been said that the wildcat is untameable. This is very largely true if it is taken some time after its eyes have opened and it has had a long association with its mother. But if taken before its eyes are open and hand-reared, it becomes as tame as any domestic cat. It can be tamed even when its eyes have been opened for several weeks, but this is a long, difficult task, and sometimes impossible. Captured as an adult, it remains wild and untameable.

As a general rule, wildcats do not take readily to prepared cat foods. They thrive best on whole prey, like rabbits, rats and mice. Wild kittens will play like domestic kittens. If they are hand-reared, the presence of humans does not worry them. If they have not been tamed, they display hostility. An adult cat, no matter how long it has been captive, distrusts man and as soon as a human being approaches, it lays back its ears, growls and displays great hostility, even ferocity. The yellow-green eyes glare, the fur rises on end and the claws are unsheathed.

Wildcats have been much persecuted and hunted over most of their range. Dogs are often used to bring them to bay in a tree or a rock where they can then be easily killed. It is a difficult animal to take alive, except in a steel trap, when it is caught by a foot and injured. No animal is easier to trap in this way. The steel trap has been illegal in the United Kingdom since 1st April, 1973. European hunters will approach a cat that has been brought to bay, with their hands and arms protected by rolls of cloth, and attempt to get it into a bag.

Although it is true to say that many cats that have become wild are frequently mistaken for true wildcats, there is no reason at all to doubt that people often see the real animal at night, especially on a mountain road, lit up by a car's headlamps, in the Highlands of Scotland. Any big, striped cat seen after dark in the Scottish Highlands is just as likely to be the real thing as an impostor.

Gloved Cat

The gloved cat (*Felis lybica*) is considered by most naturalists to be the ancestor of the domestic cat. It is about 18 inches in overall length, including a tail of 9 inches. In size, and general coat pattern, it resembles any one of a dozen types of the domestic cat. The basic coat is a more or less constant yellow or grayish-fawn on the upper part of the body, reddish on the head and along the back. The flanks are paler and the belly fur is almost white. The tiger striping is actually made up of close-set, tiny black spots. The tail is yellow at the base, white on the underside and has three dark rings. The tip is black. The gloved cat tames easily and mates readily with domestic cats.

The species is widely distributed in Africa and is also found in Arabia, Sardinia, Corsica and Majorca.

Lynxes

Lynxes are medium-sized cats, readily identifiable by their large, pointed ears, their thick-set body, long legs and stump tail.

Although lynxes are found mainly in forest habitats, they are adaptable, and occur on plains and deserts, sometimes close to human habitations. They can be as destructive as leopards, and impose a constant threat to domestic livestock. Their habits and their style of hunting are different from those of other cats.

82

The African wildcat is very common throughout the lands where the earliest cultures flourished, especially in Egypt and Arabia. It is believed to be the ancestor of the domestic cat.

Common Lynx

The common lynx (*Felis lynx*) was at one time more common and widely distributed than it is today. It is still found in Scandinavia and north Russia; elsewhere in Europe it is extremely rare. A few still survive in Greece, the Carpathians and, perhaps, in France. It ranges across Asia to eastern Siberia and south to the Himalayas, and is found in Canada and the northern forests of the United States.

Eight or more races of the lynx occur over its wide range. The Canada lynx is the biggest and the most powerful, with longer fur than other races, and it is unspotted. The lynxes of the northern United States belong to this race. The Spanish lynx is a different species, and is found only in suitable habitats in Spain and Portugal, especially in the Coto Donana of Spain. It is smaller than the northern lynx, with shorter fur, and is heavily marked with diamond spots. The surviving lynxes of the Pyrenees may be of this species, or they may be of the northern type—that is if any actually survive there.

The biggest races of the northern (common) lynx are powerful animals, ranging in size from three to three and a half feet in length plus tail of five to eight inches. Height at the shoulder is about 20 inches. Adult males weigh between 30 and 40 pounds.

The lynx is a short-coupled, stockily built cat, big-footed, with strong legs like the tiger's. It has a characteristically humped appearance because its hindlegs are longer than the forelegs. It has prominent ear tufts about two inches long, and bushy cheek tufts that lift sideways when it hisses. These adornments, together with its short body and its rabbit-posture, make the lynx unmistakable among cats.

The lynx lives farther north than any of the other cats. Its warm fur serves as a perfect protection against the bitter cold.

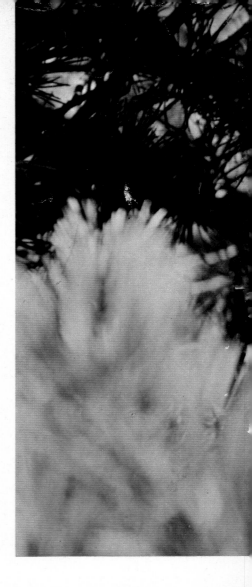

This lynx, perched at the summit of a giant cereus cactus, is inspecting its hunting territory. It is an American species known as the bobcat (Lynx rufus).

In summer the coat of lynxes varies from reddish-gray to tawny-red, spotted more or less with black; the winter coat is thicker and softer and the spots become hidden or disappear. The soles of the feet, the front of the neck and the fur round the eyes are white. The eyes are bronze, with round pupils. In general, female lynxes are browner and less boldly marked than males.

The lynx is a shy, secretive cat, elusive and not readily seen. Its main habitat is forest or thickly wooded country, rich in game and with plenty of ground cover. It is a settled species, remaining on the same range for long periods, until there is some failure of food supply or habitat upset. Consequently it is familiar with every part of its hunting ground. It is mainly a night hunter.

In North America the population of lynxes fluctuates with that of the so-called snowshoe rabbits, which are its main prey there. This synchronized fluctuation has been noted in other predator-prey relationships. In the "year of no rabbits" the north American lynxes have to change ground, and so become rare where they were numerous.

Although such a small cat—it is usually described as medium-sized—the lynx is powerful out of all proportion, and well able to kill big prey. In winter, when the drifts are deep, the lynx remains highly mobile because of its big pads, so it has a great advantage over big game in difficulty in the snow. At such times a lynx will not hesitate to attack even deer or moose.

But its normal prey consists of hares, rabbits, foxes, chipmunks, lemmings, birds, and in Canada and the northern United States, the snowshoe rabbit. It is a good swimmer and can catch fish. It will eat insects.

In the northern parts of its range the lynx hardly ever comes into conflict with man. In more temperate regions it comes into conflict with shepherds and hunters. In the Swiss Alps it kills dormice, chamois, grouse, pheasant, ptarmigan, sheep, calves, goats, marmots, hares and rabbits. Such a prey list causes it to be hunted ruthlessly by man. In one night a lynx killed more than 30 sheep.

The lynx will stalk prey. It will also climb into a tree or a rock and lie in wait. From this commanding position it leaps upon its victim. If it does not kill the prey at the first strike, it will not pursue it. When it does strike, it breaks the victim's spine, often cutting the carotid artery with a bite. After a kill, it may spend some time playing with the carcass before beginning to eat.

The hunting lynx retires at dawn and spends the daytime in a hiding place among rocks or dense undergrowth. It prefers coniferous woodlands to mixed or hardwoods, where the carpeting of pine needles hides its tracks.

The track of the lynx cannot be confused with that of any other animal. It is bigger than the wolf's, round, truncated at the front and shows no claw marks. When well printed, the track looks like a necklace of pearls. The lynx is known for its habit of backtracking—that is retracing its steps. This happens even where several lynxes are hunting together. One hunter has told the story that the first time he tracked a lynx, he saw two sets of footprints and assumed that he was following two animals. A little farther on, the two sets of tracks merged into one. He was astonished to find, on entering the clearing where the lynxes had attacked

a deer, that there had been at least four of them.

The lynx lives like no other cat because it walks wider. Despite its lack of cat-like grace and elegance, it is agile, swift and strong. It can perform tremendous leaps, as can be readily seen if one looks at its tracks in snow.

Like so many cats, the lynx is solitary outside the breeding season. The mating season is in winter but the actual period varies according to latitude. At this time the males howl and fight ferociously over the females. The gestation period is about 60 days. The female lynx gives birth to three or four young, in a hole in rocks or in an old fox den. At birth, lynx kittens weigh about ten ounces. Their eyes open when they are nine or ten days old. Once they are weaned, the female carries small mammals and birds to them and, soon afterwards, teaches them to hunt.

If caught very young, lynx kittens can be tamed easily, and remain friendly in captivity; but if they are taken adult they are unpredictable. They remain gloomy, stubborn and capricious, and cannot be trusted. They require careful

(Top)
The fur of the Canadian lynx, or polar lynx (Northern lynx) is very much longer, thicker and more supple than that of other types of lynx and, for this reason, is much sought after.

(Above)
Provided they are captured very young, lynxes are easily tamed, but they are difficult to feed in captivity as they require a varied diet of high quality food.

looking after in zoos because, although they can withstand the coldest conditions, their quarters must be completely dry and well protected from air currents.

In the Middle Ages, the lynx was found all over central Europe and was common in the Germanic forests. It was considered the most dangerous of all the cats and was persecuted with so much venom that it disappeared from these areas. The Romans occasionally used it in their circuses. The ancients credited it with great intelligence and it was considered to be superior in this respect to the wolf. It was widely believed that it was more keen-sighted than any other animal. In Germany, it occupied an important place in folklore and mythology.

Lynxes are good climbers and excellent swimmers, able to cross wide expanses of water. Contrary to popular belief, hearing is its most acutely developed sense, not sight. Its sense of smell is not highly developed. As in most of the cats, including the domestic variety, the whiskers play an important role as organs of touch.

The cry of the lynx is difficult to describe. It is full and strident, in many ways resembling the caterwauling of domestic cats. It utters a succession of high-pitched croaking sounds that deepen gradually until they become like the roar of a bear. In general, however, the lynx cries only when it is tired or hungry. When angry, it arches its back and hisses with its cheek tufts outspread. Like the domestic cat, it displays pleasure by purring.

In the northern part of its range, the lynx is hunted in a variety of ways. Traps are least effective because the lynx will often learn to avoid them. In any case, it is difficult to overpower the trapped and infuriated lynx. Hunting with dogs is sometimes tried, but dogs have to be strong and agile, with great stamina, because the lynx will twist in all directions and leap tirelessly trying to escape. This cat avoids man, but when wounded or concerned it will attack.

The lynx's fur is in considerable demand by the fur trade. Its flesh is eaten and was once considered a great delicacy, being white and not unlike veal. Among certain people, the flesh is eaten by women and tiger flesh is reserved for men.

Do not imagine that this lynx has got itself into a tricky situation. It is an excellent swimmer, able to cross the widest rivers without the slightest trouble.

Caracal (Felis caracal)

The caracal of Africa, like the bobcat of the New World, is closely related to the lynx. As a result, it is sometimes known as the African lynx or desert lynx. Among cats of its size, it is far and away the most powerful.

It is a handsome animal, standing about 18 inches tall at the shoulder. Even in small specimens, the height is about a foot. The tail measures nine inches. It is about two and a half feet long. Weight range is up to 40 pounds. As in the Northern lynx, the hind quarters are longer than the forelegs. It has the same ear tufts as the Northern lynx but it does not have the side whiskers.

The caracal is a desert or semi-desert animal. Although known as the African lynx, it is found outside Africa, its range expanding into Arabia, Afghanistan and India, where in Asia, it is becoming rarer each year.

Although it so closely resembles the Northern lynx in general appearance, the caracal has a more slender body and is an excellent runner. Its smooth, yellowish-fawn coat blends perfectly with its habitat. The stomach and the throat are almost white. On the upper lip there is a spot or a black stripe. The fur of the caracal varies from black to white according to the region in which it lives. Although the young are born spotted, the spots disappear after some months and the adults have a plain coat.

The caracal has a wide prey range. It kills small antelopes, a variety of small mammals, monkeys, lizards and birds. It can leap high and is able to catch birds on the wing. It is said that this lynx can kill snakes and it has been reported as killing an eagle. It is also able to kill sheep and goats.

It is said that the caracal is the most difficult of all cats to tame. In captivity, it never betrays the slightest sign of submission. If approached by a human being, it is at once prepared to attack, and displays great hostility. It glares with such intensity that it is not difficult to understand why people, long ago, believed its stare to be bewitching.

However untameable the caracal may be, it is a fact that it is still used in India for hunting. It is hunted against deer, antelopes, foxes and various birds. Caracals were used in India in competition not so long ago. Owners of caracals would turn the animals loose among a flock of pigeons, competing to see whose cat could kill the greatest number of birds—often as many as 12—before the flock took flight.

The short, plain coat of the caracal blends perfectly with the desert regions where it lives. Its hue is more or less dark according to its environment.

The caracal is probably the most difficult of all the cats to tame, but it can be trained for hunting, like the cheetah, and is almost as swift.

Domestic Cats

In 1758 Carl Linnaeus, (1707–78), the father of zoological classification, named the domestic cat *Felis catus* and, of course, everybody knows what a domestic cat looks like, despite the great variety of types. But its origin is still something of a mystery.

Today it is generally believed that the several varieties of short-haired domestic cats derive from *Felis lybica*, a species of wildcat found throughout Africa where it goes by many names—cafu cat, bush cat, Nubian cat, gloved cat. *Felis lybica* is the same size as a large domestic cat. It has short hair in various shades of reddish-gray, a ringed tail, and is easily tamed.

Long-haired domestic cats give rise to the same problems of origin. For a long time it was thought that these long-haired cats, collectively called Persian, were descended from *Felis manul* or Pallas's cat; but recent research has cast doubt on this. Despite their bushy tail and their long, thick coat, the body and face markings of Persian cats are quite different from Pallas's.

There appears to be one certainty, which is that the domestic cat of Europe, in spite of many similarities, is not descended from the European wildcat. In Roman times the domestic cat was rare, costly and much sought after, whereas the wildcat was common in all the forests of Europe up to the 19th century. If the domestic type had been descended from the wildcat, it would surely have been a common animal and inexpensive. It has recently been sug-

gested by Professor Harrison Matthews that domestic cats of Northern Europe, especially in a country like Scotland, may have benefited from infusions of wildcat blood by cross-breeding, and it is certainly true that the Scottish wildcat sometimes interbreeds with the domestic type.

The association of cat and man goes back to about 4000 B.C., which is not so very long ago if one thinks how much earlier many other animals have become domesticated. Excavations of prehistoric remains have discovered, beside human fossils, those of ox, goat, dog and other animals—but never any of the cat. Nor does the domestic cat appear in any cave drawings. On the other hand, it appears regularly in tomb paintings and frescoes of the first Egyptian dynasty. It is known that about 450 B.C., anyone

Cats' eyes have almond-shaped pupils which contract or dilate according to the intensity of the light.

who killed a cat in Egypt was punished by death. Four hundred years later, Diodorus of Sicily reported that a Roman soldier who had killed a cat was stoned by a furious Egyptian mob. In ancient Egypt it was customary, in case of fire, to save the domestic cat first before any attempt was made to put out the flames. When a cat died, the whole family would shave their eyebrows as a token of mourning.

Cats were held in such high esteem in Egypt that their export was forbidden, but Phoenician merchants carried on a thriving contraband trade and introduced the domestic cat to Asia Minor and eventually to Europe. The cat was domesticated in India about the same time as in Egypt. Indian women used it to guard their grain stores against rodents. To this day, the Bengal cat, or leopard cat, is easily tamed, and is probably the ancestor of the spotted cats found in India.

The Chinese knew the domestic cat before Europeans ever heard of it. The Japanese were not far behind them. In China and Japan the cat was used to protect silkworms against rats. Confucious is reputed to have owned a cat of which he was very fond. The same is recorded of the Prophet Mohammed.

Oddly enough, the Greeks do not appear to have shown much interest in cats. The Romans, on the other hand, were extremely interested in them, and it was Caesar's legions that were largely responsible for introducing cats to the rest of Europe, and particularly to England. It appears that in the 4th century A.D. the domestic cat ousted the stone-marten in Rome as a rat killer. In France the genet was the animal used as a rat killer until the cat supplanted it in the 15th century.

In the Middle Ages, cats were not very popular because of their association with witchcraft and black magic. Superstitions about cats, some of them still current today, date from this period. There are still people who suspect that the cat is a reincarnation of the devil and regard it as bad luck if a black one crosses their path. In other places there are people who consider that a black cat crossing their path brings good luck.

Cat superstitions vary from place to place. Many such superstitions are connected with the weather. Indonesians

Light, silent and infinitely patient, the cat makes an excellent hunter. Even a cat in a garden can remind one of a tiger in the jungle.

cats, for example: agile as a cat; fight like cat and dog; to let the cat out of the bag; when the cat's away the mice will play. Then there is the very trenchant Scots proverb that a "blate cat maks a prood moose".

Cats, however affectionate, are noted for their aloofness, and it is often said that the cat has an independence of spirit that the dog lacks. It has to be borne in mind that wild cats are generally solitary animals, and territorial, whereas dogs are members of a social group, of a hierarchial society, and are accustomed to a peck order. This they find in their association with man.

The cat has not been domesticated as long as the dog and accepts association with man on a different basis, never entirely giving up its right to be a free animal. It goes out when it wants, sleeps when it pleases, accepts petting and fondling when it feels like it, refuses attention when it is not in the mood, and eats when it likes. In return, the cat offers no more than its beauty and elegance. If it chases mice, it is because it likes to hunt, not because it wishes to please or to make itself useful. It will not work for those who feed it, however great its affection for them. The modern domestic cat is still quite capable of looking after itself and of obtaining its own food and shelter.

and Malays believe that if you wash your cat it will bring on rain. In western Europe it is widely believed that if a cat washes over its ears it is a sign of rain. There are sailors who believe that if a cat mews and appears cross, they will face a hard voyage, but if it is bright and lively, there will be a brisk following wind. It used to be said that a contrary wind at sea could be raised by shutting a cat in a canister. Throwing a cat overboard brought on an immediate storm. No sailor would ever dream of doing this, however, because it is considered good luck to have a cat aboard.

Occult powers are attributed to cats. It is said that they can guess man's most secret thoughts and that they have the power of hypnotism. A cat with three different hues in its coat protects one against fire and fever. To drown a cat brings seven years' bad luck. Many common expressions have reference to

)
white European cat is not an albino.
e albino cats, just as there are
most types of animals, but they have
is cat has orange eyes.

(Above)
The female cat is an attentive mother who not only feeds her kittens but watches over them continually, even when she appears to be dreaming of something quite different.

Man has tacitly accepted the cat's refusal to become a domestic slave. He has been able to breed and choose from a wide variety of dogs as pets and workers, but he has to content himself with a cat from a few varieties, all of them equally attractive and of about the same height, weight and appearance.

The cat is always a free animal, even when it is a household pet. The dog may mark its territory by raising its leg, but this has become a mechanical gesture without significance in a world where dogs and lamp-posts have multiplied enormously. One expects a dog to show hostility when a stranger approaches its master's garden, car or house. The cat's reaction is different. When it defends its master's property it is defending its own—against other cats. Everything else

is unimportant. If it marks its territory by spraying urine here and there—including on its master's bed—it is only to deter other cats.

It is thought that a male cat makes three territories for itself. The first and smallest, at the heart of the territory, is its lair or resting place where it will not tolerate the presence of another male cat. If it does allow another male cat to come near, it is because it knows it will dominate the intruder completely. The second territory surrounds the first and is less aggressively guarded. Here peaceful meetings will sometimes take place. The third territory, which is much wider, is the cat's hunting range, and here strange cats are allowed to enter without fear of attack.

Cats have a highly developed sense of

territory, and their territory is always liberally marked by urine. It is for this reason that they often suffer when their masters change house. Some cats travel considerable distances through unknown country to find their former homes. That they survive and reach their destination in good physical condition proves they can look after themselves.

If a cat is well treated and given a lot of attention, its affection for its master grows. But if it is neglected, it will react accordingly. It is quite a common thing for a cat to leave the family home in summer and take to the woods, where it quickly reverts to a wild state. When winter comes, it returns to the comforts of its old home, often accompanied, if it is a female, by kittens that have been born in the interval.

Siamese kittens are practically white when they are born. The dark parts—mask, ears, legs and tail—only appear later, together with the harsh voice that is so characteristic of the breed.

The domestic cat is a graceful, clean and friendly animal of surprising agility. It walks with light, deliberate steps, putting down its velvety paws precisely. Its retractile claws enable it to walk silently. When walking, it places the hind feet exactly on the spot located by the forefeet, as foxes do. When chased or frightened, it can move swiftly in a series of bounds but on flat, open ground, its speed cannot equal that of a dog. Consequently, when hunted, it will usually try to climb a tree or a wall.

No matter how it falls, a cat always succeeds in landing on its feet—thanks to its great sense of balance and its extraordinary ability to twist round in mid air. If it falls from a great height, its tail acts as a rudder. Cats can swim, but do so usually only in exceptional circumstances. They have been known, however, to jump into ponds to catch fish, and a cat does not hesitate to enter

(Top)
...ther pedigree or mongrel, all kittens have ...pleness nature. Independent and inquisitive, ...uilibrium, their days exploring their

(Above)
Up to the age of three months, kittens have a very small stomach, and since they cannot eat much at a time, they have to eat very frequently.

the water if her kittens are in danger.

Although cats usually sleep on their sides, they have a great sense of comfort, and will adopt any position for sleeping, including curling into a ball or lying on their backs.

The domestic cat has a wide variety of calls—mews, groans, whistles, spitting sounds and hisses to indicate pleasure, anger, surprise or fear. Most domestic cats have a special call when greeting their masters, and everyone knows that a satisfied cat purrs. The cat's miaow is kept exclusively for human beings, and is never uttered to other cats.

The senses of touch, sight and hearing are the most highly developed. That of smell is less acute. The cat's whiskers are stiff but elastic, and are highly sensitive organs of touch. It is still widely believed that it uses its whiskers to judge the width of an opening before trying to pass through it, but this is highly dubious because in the majority of domestic cats the breadth of the body

(Top)
For hundreds of years black cats have been the subject of superstitions, some of which are still current. In the Middle Ages, they were suspected of being the incarnation of the devil.

(Above)
After centuries of domestication, the cat still retains its independence and is perfectly capable of providing its own food by hunting.

erent

Whichever way it falls, a cat always ... *to land on its feet, thanks to its* ... *and remarkable sense of*

far exceeds the spread of the whiskers. The paws are equally sensitive organs of touch. Cats have excellent day and night vision. The pupils of the eyes react quickly to varying light intensity. Although the cat can see objects in very poor light, it is as blind as any other animal in total darkness.

The cat's sense of hearing is perhaps its most highly developed sense. It reacts in much the same way as people to low frequency sounds but, in the higher frequencies, it can hear sounds far beyond the range of the human ear.

To be called as fastidious and meticulous as a cat is high praise, for it is an outstandingly clean animal. It grooms its fur regularly and hides its excrement in the earth or sawdust.

The cat's complex character has resulted in its having as many detractors as supporters. Those who dislike cats call them untrustworthy, hypocritical, disloyal, thieving and unpredictable. Some cats may be some of these things, but to call any cat a hypocrite or disloyal is pure anthropomorphism and meaningless. Opinions like these are based, to a very great extent, on unfair comparison with the dog whose attributes are totally different. While dogs are noisy and demonstrative, the cat is distant and reserved. Its personality shows three main characteristics — independence, dignity and a love of solitude.

Unlike the dog, the cat has no desire to serve any master. Most cats refuse to learn to perform the simplest tricks, but are quite capable of accomplishing the most difficult feats to obtain their own ends. This independence makes the cat a difficult subject for an intelligence study. Professor Benit records an amusing story in this connection.

A cat was placed in a bell jar in which a near vacuum had been created. It was oppressed by lack of air, but soon recovered when air was let in. When it was put in the bell jar again, in a repeat experiment, the cat reacted with great intelligence. When the air current was introduced, it calmly put its paw on the inlet, but immediately withdrew it when it saw that the air was being taken away again. This experiment was repeated several times and the cat always reacted in the same way.

The cat's independent nature has given it a perfectly justifiable reputation for disobedience. Quite often a cat will finally do what one wants it to do, but it always appears as though the decision was the cat's and nobody else's.

The cat is naturally cautious and wary, not leaping before it looks. When it is put out at night, it will sit on the doorstep until its eyes become accustomed to the darkness before making a move. At threat of danger, it likes to get to a safe place, preferably off the ground, so that it can look down on its enemy. From its safe seat, it contemplates the situation,

Persian cats are pedigree house cats. As a result of selective breeding over many years for quality alone, they have gradually lost their instinct for hunting.

(Right)
In common with all cats, this young European tabby is a superb climber. When threatened by danger, the cat, not a very swift runner, prefers to climb to safety.

(Pages 98–9)
Two Persian cats, one cream, the other white. The white Persian cat has eyes of different hues, which is fairly typical.

knowing well that it is beyond reach.

But when brought to bay the cat will defend itself with the greatest courage, standing tall at full stretch with back arched and all its fur on end. This is not a reaction of fear, but a posture to make itself look bigger and so intimidate its attacker. With eyes glittering and every claw unsheathed, the cat betrays its ancestry. It is now a miniature tiger, prepared to defend itself against five or six dogs. As soon as the battle is over, which is usually when the dogs withdraw, the cat sits down and resumes its detached expression almost as though it were meditating on the absurdity of settling disputes by violence.

Nevertheless, it would be a great mistake to think that any cat can deal with one dog, let alone five or six. If the dogs really mean business, the cat is dead. Many breeds, notably greyhounds and some terriers, are specialist cat killers.

Undemonstrative though it is, the cat is capable of strong likes and dislikes. Although fundamentally a solitary beast, it can become greatly attached to a master or family. An abandoned dog will seek the company of other dogs because it is one of a naturally gregarious species; but a domestic cat, in a similar situation, will live alone, seeking out its own species only to mate.

The domestic female cat is usually mature by the age of five or six months. Unlike domestic dogs, who are on heat twice a year, cats have irregular cycles and irregular mating periods. They come on heat most frequently during the summer, and the period can last from three days to three weeks.

During the mating season, the female cat has a distinctive call that can be heard by all the males of the neighbourhood. The placid stay-at-home domestic female suddenly becomes wild and restless and takes to prowling night and day in search of a mate. Now it prefers a barn, a roof or a cellar to the comforts of home. Everybody has been wakened at some time by the caterwauling of cats, which sounds like the wailing of a child.

The males fight each other for precedence, for the female will mate with one or all of them. Contrary to popular belief, a female cat can produce, in the same litter, kittens fathered by several mates. The gestation period varies from about 56 to 69 days. Even in this, the cat obeys no set rule.

Some time in advance of the birth of her kittens, the female cat prepares her nest in a quiet place. She knows instinctively to hide her kittens away; otherwise the father would almost certainly eat them. Each kitten is born enclosed in a membrane which the mother tears by licking. The female cat is an attentive nurse and an excellent mother. Her instinct is so strong that, as a substitute for her kittens, she will nurse fox cubs, leverets, and even rats or mice.

Apart from nursing her young with great care, she spends much time licking them and grooming their fur with her

(Left)
The personality of the Siamese cat is rather similar to that of the dog. It does not mind being kept on a lead and loves to accompany its master when he goes out.

(Top)
White Persian cats can have orange or blue eyes. Those with blue eyes are usually deaf—the reason for which has yet to be discovered.

Black Persian cats often have a poor-looking coat when they are born, flecked with reddish-brown or grayish reflections, but by the time they are six months old, all the hairs should be a very deep black.

rough tongue. They grow rapidly, and soon know their mother's voice, staggering to the warmth of her body on shaky legs whenever they hear her call. Day by day, their limbs become stronger. They play a great deal and the mother joins in their play. They learn from her by watching her and make rapid progress. They develop great agility and learn how to use their claws, although at this stage they still find climbing difficult. Now the mother begins to teach them to hunt. She does this by bringing them small, live mammals on which they practise.

Despite their self-sufficiency and independence, cats often become attached to other animals, notably dogs, with which they will live in perfect harmony. It has been known for a cat to have a very friendly relationship with a parrot. It was never irritated when teased by the parrot and allowed it to peck its tail. Cats will make friends with fox cubs, leverets, birds, badger cubs—almost anything that is brought into the home.

Basically, the cat is a carnivore, with powerful jaws and sharp, pointed teeth designed for eating flesh. The domestic cat has been compelled by man to become omnivorous but, if left to itself, it quickly becomes entirely carnivorous. It would be a mistake to think that domestic cats hunt only from necessity.

They are born hunters, and a well-fed cat will still hunt mice. In fact, well-fed cats are often better mouse hunters than hungry cats.

One has only to live in a house infested by rats and mice to appreciate how useful a cat can be. It will hunt house-mice, dormice, field-mice and rats. But of these, it seems to prefer house-mice as prey. Country cats will hunt field voles which they seem to prefer to anything else.

Many cats are able to kill the biggest rats; others do not have this kind of courage. Cats kill shrews but do not eat them. It is highly likely that shrews are killed by mistake because cats continue to kill them long after they have discovered that they do not like them. Cats also eat lizards, grass snakes, spiders, grasshoppers, cockchafers and many other insects. They hunt rabbits, and many country cats maintain themselves on this prey. Most cats hunt birds, seem-

As in the case of Siamese cats, the International Cat Association recognizes several different breeds of colourpoints.

(Top)
The colourpoint is a Persian cat with the hues of the Siamese, produced by careful selective breeding. It has a light body, dark extremities and blue eyes.

(Right)
Tortoiseshell cats have patches of three different hues on their coat. They are nearly always females. Male tortoiseshell cats are rare and always sterile

ingly more for sport than anything else. But cats can be taught not to hunt birds and to leave poultry alone. Some cats have a habit of stealing from the larder. This is true even of well-fed cats and may be due partly to boredom.

Despite their heavy predation on mice and rats, cats are unable to reduce the population of either, which is true of most carnivores. They live, as it were, on the interest of the mouse population, not on the capital. Nevertheless, they take a heavy toll of small rodents, and some big adult cats are able to eat up to 20 mice in a day.

There is a legend relating that when Noah built his ark, he had two of everything except the cat, which was unknown at that time. The rain began to fall and the rats and mice began to multiply so that the ark's provisions dwindled alarmingly. Noah, in despair, asked the lion for advice. The lion thought, scratched his head and sneezed, whereupon two little lions jumped out of his nostrils. These were the first cats. They began hunting immediately and the number of rats and mice quickly dwindled. The terrified survivors raced away to hide in holes and never ap-

peared again. The cats became popular.

The cat demonstrates its skill as a hunter by its ability to attack poisonous snakes, such as vipers, and even rattlesnakes. It strikes with its claws and nearly always succeeds in avoiding attack from the snake. It never makes a frontal approach but stalks round and round the snake, which eventually becomes too tired to be wary. At that moment, the cat strikes, leaping to one side almost at the same moment to avoid the snake's counter-strike. This attack and counter-attack may go on for an hour before the snake is finally killed. But it is not eaten.

Cats are divided into two main groups: long-haired and short-haired. The long-haired varieties are now known by the general term Persian, while the short-haired varieties have two distinct branches—European and foreign.

The Persian cat first appeared in Europe at the end of the 16th century and is considered by many people to be the feline aristocrat. There is great variety in hue, but all Persian cats have a long, thick, silky, shining coat. They have a collar of hair forming a frill that extends down between the front paws. The tail is short and thick. The skull is broad, the eyes large and round, and the ears small and hairy. The nose is short, the cheeks full and the jaw flat. The body is stocky and solidly built, the legs short and strong.

Persian cats can be of one or several hues. The white Persian, sometimes

Man has taken the cat all over the world and attitudes towards cats vary. Some people treat them with indifference; others regard them as pleasing companions; yet others look on them as beautiful animals to be exhibited at shows; while others keep them merely as mouse hunters. In China and Manchuria, cats are fattened for the table, and are regarded as a great delicacy. In Thailand and Burma they are still looked upon as gods.

The cat's wide distribution in the world (it occurs everywhere except the Polar regions and the High Andes) together with its vagabond nature and pioneering spirit, have resulted in wide variations of hue and other features, such as eyes and ears.

Rules for the breeding and controlled reproduction of domestic cats were laid down in England, where the first cat show was held in 1871. The credit for creating today's recognized breeds of cats must, therefore, go to Britain. Even today, strict selection is practised to improve strains. America and Europe followed Britain's example. Interest in cat breeding has grown and cat clubs have sprung up everywhere, most of them affiliated to the International Cat Association. When one type of cat shows definite characteristics, repeated through several generations, a particular breed is considered to be established.

(Top)
The sacred cat of Burma has the shape of a Persian cat combined with the hues of the Siamese, but its paws are white and its base is golden.

called the Angora, is not an albino. True albinos have pink eyes, whereas the white Persian has eyes of orange or blue. White Persians with blue eyes are more delicate than those with orange eyes and often suffer from deafness.

Tortoiseshell Persians are of three hues: black, red and cream. There is also a variety that is tortoiseshell and white. These cats are nearly always female. Males are rare and always sterile. A tortoiseshell female is crossed with one of the three basic hues. But the hue of the kittens is unpredictable, so tortoiseshell Persians remain quite rare.

The Persian chinchilla is perhaps the most attractive cat of all. It is a white-furred cat with black-tipped hairs that give it an overall silvery appearance. The smokey Persian has white fur, tipped with black, but the black tips are confined to its back, head and feet. It is

white on the chest, sides and ear tufts.

Persian cats may also be mottled black or brown, russet or silvery. Because of the length of their coat, it is always more difficult to distinguish the contrasting marks of Persians.

The colourpoint Persian is the most recent type evolved by breeders. It has been officially recognized only since 1955, but its popularity is growing.

For many years, breeders tried to produce a long-haired Siamese, but results were unsatisfactory. The Siamese just didn't look right with long hair, which concealed its sleek elegance. By crossing this new Siamese with the Persian, it was hoped that the Siamese body hue might be transferred to the Persian. But the shape and hue of the eyes still present problems to breeders. The perfect specimen must have the intense sapphire blue eyes of the Siam-

ese, but at the same time must be large and round as in the Persian.

The sacred cat of Burma resembles the colourpoint. One legend relates that long ago, before the birth of Buddha, there lived in the mountains of Indo-China an old man who owned a white cat. When the old man thought that his death was near, he lay down to await it at the feet of a golden idol that had eyes as blue as sapphires. The cat squatted on its master's head. When the old man died, his soul passed into the cat's body. The cat's fur turned to gold like the statue and its eyes became as blue as sapphires. Only the tips of its paws remained white where they had touched the head of its dead master.

The common short-haired cat is a strong, well-built animal. It is shapely, with a broad chest. It has a tapering tail, broad and thick at the base. The legs are

(Left)
The Chartreuse cat is big and strong with a short snout, wide ears and round cheeks. Its plain coat is lavender-gray.

There are two types of tabby coats: striped (like the tiger) and marbled (mottled). These two patterns are never found together in one animal.

105

strong, the ears widely spaced, the eyes round, the cheeks full, the muzzle snubbed and the nose flat. The hair is short, fine and smooth. The vast army of stray cats and alley cats that make up the great majority of the cat population belong to this group.

As with Persians, there is a wide variety of hues in the short hairs. The white cat is no more an albino than the Persian, and it is just as deaf if it has blue eyes. The black cat is a pure breed despite all arguments to the contrary. Black domestic cats are very rarely totally black, and always have green eyes. The true black European has orange eyes without a trace of green and a jet-black coat with no hint of red in it. Striped and brindled cats usually go under the name of tabbies at cat shows. Their markings are black on a brown or silver base or chestnut on a reddish base.

The Carthusian cat is big and strong with a short muzzle and broad ears. Formerly this cat was either slate-gray or violet, but breeders have succeeded in evolving a beautiful lavender strain with amber eyes.

The Manx cat is quite different from all other breeds. It has no tail. Its back is short and its sides and hind quarters are higher than the rest of its body. It moves in leaps rather like a rabbit. Its head is large and round without being snubbed like the Persian's. Because of its prominent cheeks, its nose appears short. Its ears

(Top)
The Siamese cat is the best known of the short-haired exotic cats. Its slim body is in perfect proportion.

(Above)
The Abyssinian cat does not come from Abyssinia. It has been created by English breeders.

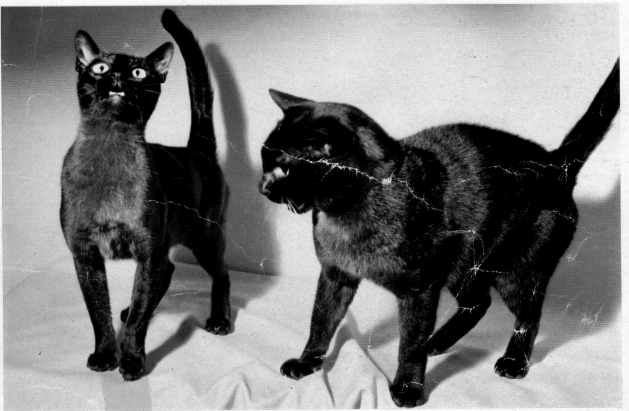

(Top)
The very short, dense and glossy hair of the Russian Blue resembles the skin of the seal. The coat is a beautiful blue and its eyes are green.

(Above)
The Burmese cat, of average size, has longer hindlegs than forelegs, and a warm-hued, plain coat, sable or blue.

are broad at the base and taper to a point. For show purposes, absence of a tail must be total. A stump is not good enough. There must be a slight depression at the spot where the tail of other cats usually begins. The rump of a Manx cat is rounded like a ball. Its coat may be of any hue.

The foreign short-haired cat is graceful, lithe and slender. The head is triangular in shape, with a broad skull and narrow muzzle. The eyes are almond-shaped and Asiatic in appearance. The ears are a distinctive feature, broad at the base and pointed at the tip. The tail is long and slender.

The best known cat of this type is probably the Siamese which is one of the most svelte and elegant, a true aristocrat. It has a pale body with dark points—muzzle, ears, paws and tail. The International Cat Association recognizes five varieties of Siamese according to hue combinations. The Siamese is the one cat whose personality most closely resembles that of the dog. It will go walking on a lead and likes to accompany its master wherever he goes. It has a unique cry and is often noisy.

The Abyssinian cat has a brown or reddish coat with two or three black bands near the rump. It is a fairly small cat with large, expressive eyes, a narrow head and big ears.

The Russian blue, formerly called the archangel cat, has a short, dense, shining coat that looks like sealskin. The body of this cat is slender, long and lithe. The medium-sized Burmese cat has forelegs shorter than its hindlegs. There are two types of Burmese, the sable and the blue.

The chestnut or Havana cat resembles the Burmese, but is more slender, with beautiful chestnut fur all over.

Lastly, the cat Rex, does not belong to any particular group. Until quite recently, cats had either long hair or short hair; but the hair was always smooth. The cat Rex has a mixture of long and short hairs and each hair is curled. This hair can, of course, be produced in any variety of cat and any breed that grows such hair retains all its other breed characteristics.

The Chestnut or Havana cat is more slender than the Burmese. As its name suggests, it has a beautiful chestnut coat.